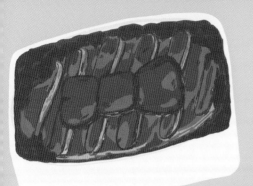

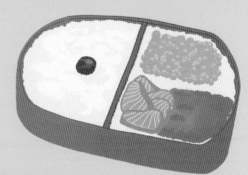

50+ Delicious Recipes Inspired by Your
Favorite Japanese Animated Films

THE
UNOFFICIAL
STUDIO
GHIBLI
COOKBOOK

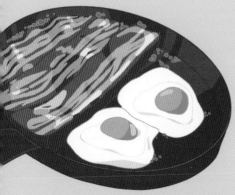

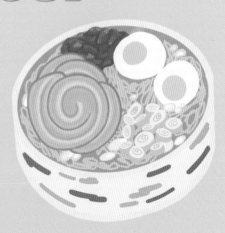

JESSICA YUN

ULYSSES
PRESS

*To those who find a bit of magic when watching the Studio Ghibli films
as well as to all the foodie enthusiasts who follow my food journey.*

*And to my two late grandmothers, who both loved to cook—
they would be proud of my debut cookbook.*

Published by:
ULYSSES PRESS
PO Box 3440
Berkeley, CA 94703
www.ulyssespress.com

ISBN: 978-1-64604-329-3
Library of Congress Control Number: 2021946580

Printed in China
4 6 8 10 9 7 5

Acquisitions editor: Casie Vogel
Managing editor: Claire Chun
Editor: Renee Rutledge
Proofreader: Michele Anderson
Front cover and interior design: Raquel Castro
Production: what!design @ whatweb.com
Photographs: © Jessica Yun
Cover illustrations: Cathy Phung
Interior illustrations: shutterstock.com

CONTENTS

INTRODUCTION   5

The Magic of Studio Ghibli   5

How to Use This Book   5

Fun Facts about Studio Ghibli   6

Special Ingredients and
Equipment   6

Chapter 1 Breakfast   9

Skillet Bacon and Eggs   11

Thyme-Infused Egg on Toast   12

A Witch's Secret to Magical
Fluffy Pancakes   15

Breakfast over Yokohama Port   16

Morning Miso Soup   17

Decadent Hot Mocha   18

Chapter 2 Lunch   19

On-the-Go Ham Sandwich   20

Haaaaaaaam Ramen   21

Iconic School Lunch Bento   22

"Save Our Building" School Bento   24

Open-Faced Cheese
and Onion Sandwich   26

Seaside Seafood Sashimi Platter   28

Mackerel Braised in Miso   31

Chapter 3 Dinner   32

Grandma's Herring and Pumpkin Pot Pie   33

Secret Message Fried Mackerel   36

Date Night Pan-Seared Salmon
in Beurre Blanc Sauce   38

Chorizo Spaghetti Bolognese   40

Chicken Congee (Okayu)   42

Hearty Beef Stew to Feed a Crowd   45

Japanese Cream Stew   46

Crystal Skin Taiwanese
Dumpling (Ba Wan)   49

Chapter 4 Snacks and Street Food 51

Classic Tempura Selection   52

Ten-don (Tempura Rice Bowl)   55

Trio of Onigiri   56

Menchi Katsu   59

Smoky and Sweet Yakitori   61

Takoyaki   63

Yakisoba Pan   65

Crispy Pork Gyoza   68

Chicken Karaage   71

Okonomiyaki   72

Tonkatsu   75

Katsudon   76

Chapter 5 Desserts and Bakery Treats 78

Hot Honeyed Milk   79

Rewarding and Decadent
Chocolate Cake   81

Tea Party Spritz Cookies   85

Tea Party Mini Gelatin   86

Tea Party Cantonese Egg Cake   87

Cheese and Onion Fish Crackers   88

Tuna Fish Crackers
(for Your Feline Friends)   90

Duo Thumbprint Cookies   91

Siberia Cake   93

Red Bean Bao   95

Pumpkin Bread   98

Black Cat Icebox Shortbread Cookies   100

Red Bow Icebox Shortbread Cookies   102

Curry Bread (Kare Pan)   103

Red Bean Croissant   106

Mini Swedish Princess Cake   111

Mini Swedish Almond Coffee Cake   114

Swedish Cardamom Buns   116

Ham and Cheese Breadsticks   119

Green Tea Melon Pan Stuffed
with Blueberry Compote   120

Japanese Soufflé Cheesecake   122

CONVERSIONS   124

RECIPE INDEX   125

ACKNOWLEDGMENTS   127

ABOUT THE AUTHOR   128

INTRODUCTION

The Unofficial Studio Ghibli Cookbook is my debut cookbook, with recipes that transform iconic foods from popular Studio Ghibli films into reality. As a qualified epidemiologist, I've turned to cooking as my stress-reliever and breakaway from the public health realm. This opportunity to share great food inspired by the iconic stories produced by Studio Ghibli combines two of my greatest loves: art and cooking. It has also taught me to appreciate a range of foods of other cultures, including Japanese, Italian, and Swedish dishes. I hope this cookbook will inspire you to go out into the kitchen and enjoy that bit of magic in cooking.

The Magic of Studio Ghibli

Studio Ghibli, the acclaimed animation film studio, was founded in 1985 in Tokyo by Hayao Miyazaki, Isao Takahata, and Toshio Suzuki. Studio Ghibli is widely known for its exceptional filmmaking and artistry, for which it has won both critical and popular praise. Studio Ghibli has captivated moviegoers with fantastic stories of magic, adventure, friendship, and family.

In 1996, The Walt Disney Company and the Tokuma Shoten Publishing Company, which controls Studio Ghibli, formed a partnership, making Disney the sole international distributor of the world-renowned animated films. One of the successful films produced by Studio Ghibli animation is *Princess Mononoke*, which was released in Japan in 1997 and in the United States two years later. The 2002 film *Spirited Away* was named the best animated feature at the Hong Kong Film Awards and received the Golden Bear, the top prize at the Berlin International Film Festival.

Food is a critical feature in Studio Ghibli productions, as every film showcases scenes of the characters cooking, eating, and sharing the most mouthwatering animated food. These scenes have symbolic meaning in line with the characters' story lines. For example, in *Spirited Away*, Chihiro is shown eating a red bean bao, symbolizing comfort and a sense of belonging that accompanies going back home. The attention to these cooking scenes makes the animated worlds of Studio Ghibli come to life, closely tying food and eating with family and emotion. I hope this cookbook brings that bit of magic from the screen to the real world for you.

How to Use This Book

This cookbook is organized in the Breakfast, Lunch, Dinner, Snacks and Street Food, and Desserts and Bakery Treats categories. While the dishes featured in this cookbook mainly consist of Japanese cuisine, they are also inspired by international foods that are showcased in the films. Ingredient substitutions are mentioned either in the Special Ingredients and Equipment section or in the tip box under each recipe. Just like animations, cooking is also an art, so I highly encourage you to add your own spin to the dishes.

Airplanes are a recurring theme of the films because Hayao Miyazaki's dad was the director of Miyazaki Airplanes, a manufacturer of fighter planes.

The word *Ghibli* is Italian for "hot winds from the Sahara Desert," referencing the aim to blow new wind through the anime industry. "Ghibli" was also the name of the Italian World War II airplane. Thus, it represents Miyazaki's love for planes.

Spirited Away is the highest-grossing film in Japanese cinema and is the only non-English film to win an Academy Award for Best Animated Feature.

Most Studio Ghibli films consist of hand-drawn animation, and Miyazaki himself hand-drew the water in *Ponyo*. However, computer animation was used in some of the films to enhance particular scenes. *Earwig and the Witch*, directed by Goro Miyazaki, the son of Hayao Miyazaki, was the studio's first full-length computer-generated imagery (CGI) movie

Despite *Nausicaä of the Valley of the Wind* being archived with other famous Studio Ghibli films, it was produced a year before the Japanese studio was established.

Special Ingredients and Equipment

Although most of the recipes in this book can be successfully made using utensils available in a well-equipped Western kitchen, there are a few ingredients and utensils worth investing in. The following can be found at your local Asian grocery market or online.

Essential Utensils

BAMBOO SUSHI MAT: Used for rolling sushi, a sushi mat ensures that the rice or tamago (rolled omelet) is firmly packed so it does not fall apart.

RICE PADDLE: A small, flat plastic or bamboo rice paddle is used to turn and fluff up cooked rice.

SKEWERS: Japanese kitchens contain an assortment of metal skewers that are used for grilling vegetables or meats. Even though you can use bamboo skewers, metal ones are a good investment as they retain the heat and keep your food warmer longer.

LACQUERED BOWL: Fine tableware is common in a Japanese kitchen, so I highly suggest investing in at least one lacquered bowl with a dome lid for soups (especially since this was featured in *Ponyo*).

MINI SAUCE DISHES: Sauces such as soy sauce, sweet chili sauce, and more, are often served in tiny dishes. Entrées may be served on a porcelain plate with a special compartment that can accommodate a variety of dish shapes and sizes for the sauce. Alternatively, these mini dishes can be placed next to the porcelain plate. I have personally started a collection of mini sauce dishes, as the designs are endless.

Essential Ingredients

BONITO FLAKES: Bonito flakes consist of dried mackerel that has been thinly sliced. This is a main ingredient for dashi.

DAIKON: This giant white radish has a multitude of uses in Japanese cuisine. It is typically served with deep-fried foods to counteract the greasiness and can be simmered with other ingredients to make an amazing one-pot meal.

DASHI STOCK: Dashi is a Japanese soup stock that can be made by simmering 1½ cups dried bonito flakes, 1 (6 x 5-inch) piece of dried kelp/seaweed in 4½ cups of water for 20 minutes. This soup base provides the pinnacle of flavor; however, not everyone has time to make it for every meal. Fortunately, various types of instant dashi powder are available, convenient for those busy days.

DRIED KELP/SEAWEED: This is much thicker compared to nori and typically requires rehydration before cooking or eating. It comes in thick sheets at the local Asian grocery store. The two types of dried seaweed commonly used in Japanese cuisine are kombu and *wakame*. Wakame, or sea lettuce, has a strong salty flavor with a subtle hint of sweetness and is used in salads or soups. In comparison, kombu is dehydrated kelp that is almost black in color with specks of white powder. This is a main ingredient in making dashi stock; it can also be eaten.

SWEET PICKLED GINGER: Perhaps best known as a side dish with sushi, pickled ginger is also used as a flavor booster, especially for *yakisoba*, or fried noodles.

MIRIN: A golden cooking wine with a very low alcohol content, gives a distinct, mildly sweet taste to simmered stocks, glazes, and dipping sauces.

MISO: This rich, savory paste is made from fermented soybeans, rice, and other grains. Use miso as a flavoring for basic dressings and simmered or grilled foods. Red miso has a thicker texture. It is used for richer soups and for general cooking purposes. White miso, which is milder, sweeter and made with a higher proportion of rice, is used for sauces and light miso soups. If you are unable to find miso paste, fish sauce is a great alternative.

NORI: Nori is tightly packed seaweed that has been dehydrated and is typically used to make sushi. When mixed with other spices, nori is also used to flavor rice.

NEUTRAL-FLAVORED OIL: These are cooking oils that are mostly flavorless and are typically suitable for deep frying and baking. Vegetable oil, canola oil, avocado oil, and grapeseed oil are good choices. Avoid stronger-flavored oils such as olive oil and sesame oil.

SESAME OIL: A prized ingredient in my household, this oil enhances food with a slight nuttiness. This is primarily used as a flavoring for dressings rather than a cooking oil due to its strong flavor and its relatively expensive cost.

SOY SAUCE: Made from fermented soybeans and wheat, soy sauce is a key ingredient in most Asian recipes; it provides an umami flavor to dishes.

TOFU: Tofu is one of the most common ingredients in Japanese cooking. It has a delicate flavor and is a great source of vegetable protein. The best tofu is made fresh every day and is sold in large blocks in a bucket of fresh water. If you are unable to find fresh tofu, look in the refrigerator section of your grocery store for water-packed tofu that is white and does not have any discoloration. Tofu ranges in texture from silken to firm. Silken tofu is ideally used for making smoothies and sauces. Soft tofu is recommended for soups and frying. Medium or firm tofu is ideal for stir-frying or grilling.

TOGARASHI: This mixture consists of seven spices, including red chile pepper flakes, *sansho* or Sichuan peppercorns, dried mandarin orange peel, white and black sesame seeds, nori slivers, and ground ginger. However, this can vary from brand to brand. You can find it in most Japanese or other Asian stores.

UMEBOSHI: This is a Japanese pickled plum, often used as a condiment in bento boxes.

CHAPTER 1
BREAKFAST

SKILLET BACON AND EGGS

1 tablespoon neutral-flavored oil, such as canola oil

7 ounces thick-cut bacon or toucinho

4 large eggs

salt and pepper, to taste

4 cups water

2 to 4 teaspoons Jasmine tea leaves or any tea of your choice

loaf of ciabatta or any crusty bread of choice, sliced

1 (3.5-ounce) wedge Maasdam cheese or any cheese of choice

This recipe is inspired by one of my favorite Studio Ghibli films about a spiteful witch, a curse, and a moving castle. You'll have to cook it without the help of your favorite fire demon, but it'll be a delicious and mouthwatering breakfast all the same. Make sure to use thick-cut bacon so you get as much grease as possible. I like to use *toucinho* (thick cuts of Portuguese-style smoked bacon). Serve with a hot bowl of tea, and you'll feel like you've just woken up in a magical castle!

Yield: 2 to 4 servings | Prep time: 0 minutes | Cook time: 20 minutes

1. Heat the oil in a large cast-iron pan over medium heat.

2. Add the bacon to the pan and fry until it is crispy on both slides, about 5 to 10 minutes.

3. Move the bacon to the sides of the pan. Crack the eggs directly into the same pan and cook until the egg whites are set, about 3 to 4 minutes. Season with salt and pepper.

4. In an electric kettle or a small saucepan, heat the water to a boil.

5. Add 1 teaspoon of tea leaves and the boiling water to each bowl (use 2 to 4 bowls, depending how many people you are feeding). Let the tea steep for 3 minutes.

6. Serve all the bacon and eggs family style (in one pan) accompanied with the crusty slices of bread, a hunk of Maasdam cheese or your cheese of choice, and bowl of green tea. This meal can be shared among a small family.

THYME-INFUSED EGG ON TOAST

2 slices fresh white bread or any bread of choice

2 tablespoons salted butter

1 tablespoon olive oil

2 sprigs fresh thyme, divided

2 large eggs

salt and pepper, to taste

1 clove garlic, peeled

This thyme-infused egg served on a thick slice of bread is a great fireside meal when you're starving, especially in a faraway place hidden in the clouds. Sharing with robots is permitted!

Yield: 2 servings | Prep time: 3 minutes | Cook time: 10 minutes

1. Pop the bread into the toaster.

2. While the bread is toasting, place the butter and olive oil in a medium pan over medium heat. Strip the leaves from the thyme stalks and set aside.

3. Once the butter has melted, add the thyme leaves (reserving a pinch for garnishing) and sauté until the mixture is aromatic. This should take a few seconds to 1 minute.

4. Crack the eggs into the same pan and cook, spooning the thyme-infused butter over the eggs until the egg whites are set, approximately 3 to 4 minutes.

5. Once the egg whites have set, turn off the heat and cover the pan with a lid for 1 minute. This will steam the egg yolk and cover it with a thin white film. Season the eggs with salt and pepper.

6. Once the slices of bread are golden brown, rub the raw clove of garlic lightly on the crusty bread. Using a spatula, transfer the eggs onto the slices of bread. Make sure to spoon the remaining butter from the pan onto the bread.

7. Garnish with the remaining thyme.

8. Divide the toast between 2 small plates, serve, and enjoy immediately.

TIP: *To get a picture-perfect, fully cooked egg on toast, use a toothpick and carefully peel away the thin white film from the egg yolk.*

TIP: *Substitute the thyme by adding chopped fresh basil, parsley, or lemon zest to your pan of melted butter before frying your eggs.*

A WITCH'S SECRET TO MAGICAL FLUFFY PANCAKES

3 tablespoons salted butter, plus extra for serving

2 tablespoons olive oil

1 small vine cherry tomatoes

½ teaspoon dried mixed herbs, such as Robertsons Mixed Herbs or Italian seasoning

salt and pepper, to taste

1½ cups all-purpose flour

¼ cup superfine sugar

½ teaspoon salt

3 teaspoons baking powder

½ teaspoon baking soda

1¼ cups buttermilk

1 large egg

1 teaspoon vanilla extract

4 tablespoons neutral-flavored oil, divided

1 smoked kielbasa sausage

maple syrup, for serving

This is the ideal breakfast before a long day of delivery work on your broomstick. Sausage and blistered tomatoes really round out this morning meal, which will surely bring your magic powers back if you've been feeling under the weather!

Yield: 2 servings | Prep time: 7 minutes | Cook time: 35 minutes

1. Melt the butter in the microwave for 1 to 2 minutes. Allow it to cool completely while you prepare the rest of your ingredients.

2. Drizzle the olive oil over the vine of tomatoes in a small bowl, then season it with the dried mixed herbs or Italian seasoning, salt, and pepper. Roast the tomatoes on the grill or under the broiler for 6 to 8 minutes, until the tomatoes start to blister.

3. In a medium mixing bowl, combine the flour, sugar, salt, baking powder, and baking soda until the ingredients are well mixed.

4. Make a well in the center of the flour mixture. Add the buttermilk, egg, vanilla extract, and melted butter.

5. Whisk until the batter is well mixed; it may be slightly thick and lumpy. If the batter is too dry, add 1 to 2 tablespoons of extra buttermilk to the batter and stir. The batter should be slightly thick and should pour easily.

6. Heat 1 tablespoon of neutral-flavored oil in a medium nonstick frying pan over medium-high heat. Add a scoop of pancake batter to the pan and cook each side for 3 to 4 minutes, until lightly golden brown. Repeat with the rest of the batter, making 4 large pancakes (4 to 5 tablespoons per pancake) or 10 mini-pancakes (2 tablespoons per pancake).

7. While the pancakes are cooking, cook your smoked kielbasa sausage according to the package instructions.

8. Serve the pancakes hot between 2 plates, with a small slab of butter, maple syrup, the smoked sausage, and the blistered tomatoes. Enjoy immediately.

BREAKFAST OVER YOKOHAMA PORT

2 tablespoons neutral-flavored oil, divided

2 large eggs, divided

salt and pepper, to taste

6 slices country ham

2 cups thinly shredded green cabbage (shred with a mandoline slicer)

2 cups cooked jasmine rice

Morning Miso Soup (page 17)

Whether you're cooking for a crowd of hungry boarders or looking for an on-the-go breakfast before raising signal flags, this is a filling breakfast sure to please just about anyone. Serve with some Morning Miso Soup.

Yield: 2 servings | Prep time: 5 minutes | Cook time: 10 minutes

1. In a medium nonstick frying pan over medium-high heat, add 1 tablespoon of oil and crack 1 egg into the pan. Season with salt and pepper and let the egg cook for 3 minutes, or until the white is set and the edges have crisped up. Transfer the egg to a plate. Repeat with the other egg and set the eggs aside.

2. Using the same pan, fry the sliced ham over medium-high heat until it becomes crispy and slightly golden, approximately 2 minutes. Transfer the ham to a plate and set it aside.

3. Serve a fried egg on top of the ham and place shredded cabbage next to the egg on each plate. This is to be accompanied with a bowl of warm rice and a small bowl of miso soup. Enjoy with the family.

MORNING MISO SOUP

1 piece kombu or wakame seaweed (approximately 6 x 6 inches)

2 cups warm water

2 teaspoons dashi powder

2 cups boiling water

2 tablespoons white miso paste

1 block soft tofu, cubed

1 green onion, sliced

sesame seeds, toasted

This super-easy, delicious miso soup is a staple in all Japanese households and goes even better with the Breakfast Over Yokohama Port (page 16). Recommended especially when you are busy at the Newspaper Club at the Latin Quarter.

Yield: 2 servings | Prep time: 35 minutes | Cook time: 12 minutes

1. Clean the kombu or wakame by rubbing any dirt off with a damp towel. Soak the kombu in warm water for a minimum of 30 minutes.

2. While the seaweed is soaking, dissolve the dashi powder in a bowl of boiling water and set aside.

3. When the seaweed is fully hydrated, discard the water and cut the seaweed up into ½-inch strips. Place the dashi powder mixture and seaweed in a medium pot and bring the mixture to a boil over medium heat, approximately 7 minutes.

4. Place the miso paste in a soup ladle and lower it into the pot until the water partially covers the miso paste. Dissolve the miso paste in the water using a pair of chopsticks and return the liquid from the ladle back into the pot.

5. Keep the miso soup at a simmer and gently add the tofu. Let the soup boil for 3 to 5 minutes.

6. Spoon the miso soup into 2 small porcelain bowls. Garnish the soup with chopped green onion and toasted sesame seeds.

TIP: *If you are using dashi granules, use 1 teaspoon of dashi granules per cup of boiling water.*

DECADENT HOT MOCHA

2 tablespoons unsweetened cocoa powder, plus more for serving

1½ tablespoons brown sugar

2 tablespoons fresh cream

1 cup whole milk

2 ounces dark chocolate (70% cocoa), chopped into small pieces

¼ teaspoon vanilla extract

2 teaspoons instant coffee

¼ cup hot water

pinch of salt

5 tablespoons fresh cream, whipped to stiff peaks

mini-marshmallows, for serving

This creamy, homemade hot mocha is known to bring comfort to trainee-witches arriving in a seaside town! Serve with any of the irresistible baked breads and cookies found in the Desserts and Bakery Treats chapter.

Yield: 1 serving | Prep time: 5 minutes | Cook time: 5 minutes

1. Combine all the ingredients except the whipped cream and marshmallows, in a medium pot over medium heat. Bring the mocha to a boil while whisking constantly, until the sugar and chocolate have melted completely, 3 to 4 minutes. Be careful not to burn the milk and chocolate, which may stick to the bottom of the pot.

2. Transfer your hot mocha to a large mug and top with the whipped cream, mini marshmallows, and a dash of cocoa powder.

3. Serve hot, accompanied with the Black Cat Icebox Shortbread Cookies (page 100).

CHAPTER 2
LUNCH

ON-THE-GO HAM SANDWICH

FOR THE HONEY MUSTARD MAYONNAISE:

1 teaspoon lemon juice

1 teaspoon honey

¼ cup Kewpie Mayonnaise

FOR THE SANDWICHES

6 slices white bread

¼ head iceberg lettuce

1 small Roma tomato, sliced

6 slices black peppered honey ham (or any ham you have available)

3 slices mild cheddar cheese

black pepper, to taste

Haaam! These sandwiches can be enjoyed on the beach with a special fishy friend or in the car when you're late for work. If you plan to share, try not to eat the ham off of them before serving them up! (Please be cautious while you eat and drive!)

Yield: 3 servings | Prep time: 15 minutes | Cook time: 0 minutes

1. For the honey mustard mayonnaise: Combine all the ingredients in a small bowl and set aside.

2. For the sandwiches: Slather the honey mustard mayonnaise onto your slices of white bread.

3. Top a slice of bread with iceberg lettuce, tomato slices, ham, and cheese.

4. Crack some fresh black pepper over the ingredients, then top the sandwich with the other slice of bread.

5. Repeat these steps for the remaining 2 sandwiches. Wrap the sandwiches in wax paper and place in a picnic basket. Serve.

HAAAAAAAAM RAMEN

2 large eggs

2 cups room-temperature water

2 packages of your favorite instant ramen noodles (I used Shin Ramyun)

4 slices black peppered honey ham (or any ham you have available)

2 green onions, sliced

Enjoy this super-comforting ramen while taking refuge in your friend's house during a dark sea storm. Dress it up with everyone's favorite deli meat: haaaaaam! Hot Honeyed Milk on page 79 is also recommended after going into a food coma with this dish.

Yield: 2 servings | Prep time: 2 minutes | Cook time: 11 minutes

1. Place your eggs in a pot of water over medium-high heat and bring the 2 cups of water to a boil. Cook the eggs for 6½ minutes for medium- to soft-boiled eggs, adjusting the heat to maintain a gentle boil.

2. Transfer the eggs to a bowl of ice water and chill until it is cold enough to handle. Gently crack your eggs all over and peel. Set the eggs aside for later.

3. Cook the noodles according to the package instructions.

4. Divide the cooked ramen noodles and the broth into 2 bowls. Slice the egg in half and place it with the sliced ham on top of the noodles. Garnish with sliced green onions.

5. For dramatic effect, place the lid over the ramen bowl and wait for the big unveiling. Enjoy!

ICONIC SCHOOL LUNCH BENTO

FOR THE SAKURA DENBU:

1 (3.5-ounce) hake fillet, sea cod, or any white fish of choice

2½ cups plus 1 tablespoon water, divided

1 drop red food coloring

½ tablespoon sugar

1 tablespoon sake

¼ teaspoon salt

FOR THE BENTO:

½ cup frozen edamame beans, shelled

2½ cups boiling water

1 whole sardine, scaled and cleaned

salt and pepper, to taste

1 tablespoon olive oil

1 cup cooked jasmine rice

1 umeboshi

When mom's away and dad deserves to sleep in, sometimes it's a big sister's job to make lunch for everyone. This is an iconic bento that includes grilled sardine, edamame beans, homemade *sakura denbu*, and umeboshi served on aromatic jasmine rice.

Yield: 1 serving | Prep time: 10 minutes | Cook time: 35 minutes

1. To make the sakura denbu: Remove the skin and bones from the fish fillet.

2. Fill a medium pot with 2½ cups water and bring to a boil.

3. Add the fish fillet to the pot and poach for 10 minutes, or until it is white and flaky.

4. Drain the fish fillet and let it cool completely.

5. Once it is cool enough to handle, gently flake the fillet with your hands. Wrap the cooked fish fillet in a cheesecloth and squeeze out any remaining liquid from the fish. While it is in the cheesecloth, flake the fish into even finer pieces with your hands. Set aside.

6. In a separate small bowl, combine the red food coloring and 1 tablespoon of water and set aside.

7. Place the flaked fish in a medium nonstick frying pan over low heat. Add the sugar, sake, salt and red food coloring mixture to the pan and stir continuously for 5 to 10 minutes—the mixture has a tendency to burn easily.

8. Once the mixture is fluffy, remove the pan from the heat and continue to stir the mixture for another minute. Set the mixture aside and let it cool.

9. For the bento: Place the edamame in a pot of boiling water and let it cook for 7 minutes, or until tender. Drain and set aside.

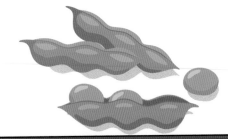

10. While the edamame is cooking, season the sardine with salt and pepper on both sides. Lightly drizzle olive oil over the fish and bake it in the oven or grill it on a barbecue grill for 5 to 7 minutes until it is fully cooked.

11. To assemble your bento box, fill three quarters of your bento box with cooked jasmine rice, ensuring that the rice covers the bottom of the box.

12. Place the grilled sardine on top of the rice in the middle of your bento (creating a division between your other rice condiments).

13. On the left-hand side of your bento box, fill one quarter of the bento box with the cooked edamame beans and the other quarter with the sakura denbu. Finally, place 1 umeboshi on top of the rice on the right-hand side of your bento box.

TIP: *Traditionally, sakura denbu is cooked codfish that has been flaked and lightly seasoned with sugar. Colored pink to represent the cherry blossom petals in Japan, it's favorite condiment for rice.*

TIP: *In the original film, shishamo, or smelt fish, is used. However, sardine is a great alternative and more accessible.*

"SAVE OUR BUILDING" SCHOOL BENTO

**FOR THE *TAMAGOYAKI*
(JAPANESE OMELET)**

3 large eggs

2 tablespoons dashi

1 teaspoon soy sauce

1 teaspoon sugar

½ teaspoon mirin

pinch of salt

2 tablespoons neutral-flavored oil

While your friends eat whatever they serve in the cafeteria, make a splash at lunchtime with this delicious homemade bento! It really isn't that hard to make and is perfect for watching goofy male classmates jump off a school building.

Yield: 1 serving | Prep time: 10 minutes | Cook time: 15 minutes

1. For the tamagoyaki, use chopsticks to whisk the eggs in a zigzag motion.

2. In a separate small bowl, combine the dashi, soy sauce, sugar, mirin, and salt.

3. Combine the egg and the dashi mixture, gently whisking until well incorporated. Pour the egg mixture into a jug with a spout for easy pouring.

4. Heat the oil in a large nonstick frying pan over low heat, then pour in ⅓ of the egg mixture, tilting the pan to cover the surface of the pan.

FOR THE STIR-FRIED SPINACH;
2 tablespoons neutral-flavored oil

1 teaspoon minced garlic

1 cup fresh spinach, chopped

½ teaspoon salt

¼ teaspoon sugar

¼ teaspoon toasted sesame oil

toasted sesame seeds, for garnishing

FOR THE BENTO:
1½ cups cooked jasmine rice

1 small kielbasa, cooked according to package instructions

1 umeboshi

1 teaspoon bonito flakes

5. Once the bottom of the egg mixture has set but is still soft, start rolling it into a log using a pair of chopsticks. Slide the omelet to one side of the pan. Add a bit more oil to the pan and pour another third of the egg mixture to cover the bottom of the pan once again. Make sure to lift the egg roll so the egg mixture spreads underneath it as well. Once the egg has been set, roll it into a log. Repeat the process for the rest of the egg mixture and set aside.

6. For the stir-fried spinach, heat the oil in a medium nonstick pan over medium heat. Add the garlic and sauté until fragrant and it is starting to brown slightly, from a few seconds to 1 minute.

7. Add the spinach and cook it down for 5 minutes, until the leaves are tender and wilted.

8. Add salt and sugar to the spinach and cook for another minute. Remove from the heat and drizzle with the toasted sesame oil. Add toasted sesame seeds for some crunch.

9. To assemble the bento, spread a thin layer of cooked jasmine rice into the bento box. Place the kielbasa on top of the rice in the middle of your bento (creating a division between your other rice condiments). Fill the bottom right-hand side of the bento with the stir-fried spinach. Slice the tamagoyaki into 1-inch rounds and place them in the top-right corner of the bento box. Add the umeboshi and bonito flakes on top of the rice, on the left side of the bento box.

10. Serve warm or at room temperature.

TIP: *Use chopsticks to ensure that the eggs are not overmixed.*

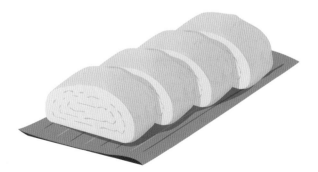

OPEN-FACED CHEESE AND ONION SANDWICH

2½ tablespoons finely chopped fresh flat-leaf parsley

½ teaspoon chile flakes

½ cup (or 1 stick) salted butter, softened

loaf of rye bread or any crusty bread of choice, sliced

3.5 ounces Gouda cheese or any mild to strong cheese, sliced

1 small red onion, sliced thinly

The simplest cheese and onion sandwich will get me through the day, especially when working in the farmlands. Even wizards need to take a break to regain their strength and enjoy lunch! Just keep an eye out for those pesky dragons.

Yield: 3 to 6 servings | Prep time: 35 minutes | Cook time: 2 minutes

1. Place the parsley, chile flakes, and softened butter in a medium bowl and stir until well combined. Spoon the mixture onto a piece of plastic wrap or parchment paper and roll it into a log. Twist the ends to seal, and refrigerate for at least 30 minutes.

2. Meanwhile, toast your bread slices in a toaster.

3. To assemble, spread the compound parsley butter onto a slice of toast. Add a slice of cheese and a thin slice of red onion on top. Repeat to make the remaining sandwiches.

4. Enjoy while taking a break from a hard day's work.

TIP: *Get creative when making your own compound butter. Some great combinations include garlic and parsley, lemon zest and chives, honey and butter, and smoked paprika and garlic.*

SEASIDE SEAFOOD SASHIMI PLATTER

FOR THE SHRIMP CEVICHE:
6 medium fresh tiger prawns, deveined and shelled, with heads and tails on

⅓ cup freshly squeezed lemon juice

FOR THE *SHIME SABA* (CURED MACKEREL):
1 medium fresh mackerel fillet

½ cup kosher salt

pinch of sugar

¾ cup rice wine vinegar

FOR THE EDAMAME SALAD:
½ cup cooked edamame beans, shelled

¼ cup sliced black olives

½ cup cubed feta cheese

½ cup halved English cucumber slices

½ cup halved cherry tomatoes

2 cups roughly chopped iceberg lettuce leaves

FOR THE VINAIGRETTE:
2 tablespoons rice wine vinegar

2 teaspoons olive oil

2 teaspoons honey

½ teaspoon chile flakes

1 teaspoon soy sauce

1 teaspoon sesame oil

This delightfully fresh seafood platter is an absolute must when going to a fancy seaside dinner party with a special blond friend.

Yield: 3 to 5 servings | Prep time: 3 hours, 15 minutes | Cook time: 5 minutes

1. Add the shrimp and lemon juice to a small ceramic bowl and toss, making sure the lemon juice covers the majority of the shrimp. Place the shrimp in the fridge and let them marinate for about 30 minutes, until the shrimp turn pink and opaque. Once the shrimp have turned pink, rinse them under cold water and pat dry. Set aside.

2. For the shime saba, rinse the mackerel fillet and pat dry. Ensure that there are no bones in the fillet by running your fingers on the surface to check for any abrasiveness. Use a pair of tweezers to pull out any bones. Cover the mackerel fillet with salt and place it in the fridge for 1 hour. The salt will cure the fish and draw out most of the moisture while keeping it firm.

3. After 1 hour, rinse the fillet under cold water and pat dry with a paper towel. In a separate bowl, mix the sugar and vinegar until the sugar dissolves.

4. Set the fillet in a medium bowl and pour the vinegar mixture over it. Place the fish back into the fridge and let it cure for 2 hours, or until the fish turns slightly opaque. This process "cooks" the fish. After 2 hours, rinse the fillet under cold water and pat dry. Set aside.

5. To make the edamame salad, combine all the salad ingredients in a large bowl and set aside. To make the vinaigrette, whisk all the ingredients in a small bowl until the honey has dissolved.

6. For the pan-seared scallops, separate the scallops from the shell and season on both sides with salt and pepper. Reserve one of the scallop shells for presentation.

7. In a large nonstick frying pan, heat the olive oil over medium heat. Add the scallops to the pan and cook for 2 minutes on each side, or until a golden crust has formed on each side. While the scallops are cooking, add the butter to the pan. Once the butter has melted, tilt the pan to one side, spoon the butter over the scallops, and continue to cook. Once the scallops are cooked, set them aside in a dish or place all of them in one of the reserved scallop shells. Add the lemon, garlic, and parsley to

FOR THE PAN-SEARED SCALLOPS:
¼ pound scallops, about 5 large scallops in shells

salt and pepper, to taste

1 tablespoon olive oil

2 tablespoons salted butter

juice of 1 lemon

2 cloves garlic, minced

1 tablespoon fresh chopped parsley

1 (3.5-ounce) fresh salmon fillet

1 (3.5-ounce) fresh tuna fillet

lemon slices

the remaining butter in the pan. Sauté until the garlic is fragrant and slightly brown. Spoon the butter parsley sauce on top of scallops.

8. To assemble on a large plate, place your ceviche shrimp in an upright position. Using a sharp sushi knife, slice the fresh salmon, tuna, and shime saba at a 45-degree angle into ½-inch-thick pieces. Place the salmon, tuna, and shime saba on the plate next to the shrimp. Lastly, add the scallops to the plate. Do not forget to add lemon slices across the plate.

9. Serve the seafood sashimi platter with soy sauce and the edamame salad dressed with your homemade vinaigrette.

TIP: *Ensure that the mackerel, tuna, and salmon are fresh and of sushi-grade quality.*

TIP: *You can also use a very sharp knife when cutting the salmon, tuna, and shime saba into slices, but I recommend investing in a sushi knife. Sushi knives are more flexible and easier to use than regular kitchen knives.*

MACKEREL BRAISED IN MISO

FOR THE MISO-BRAISED MACKEREL:

2 skin-on mackerel fillets

salt, to taste

1 cup dashi (see the tip on page 17)

2 tablespoons sake

2½ tablespoons peeled and thinly sliced ginger

3 tablespoons sugar

5 tablespoons red miso paste

FOR THE SOY-BRAISED DAIKON RADISH:

1 (3.5-ounce) daikon radish, peeled and cut into 1-inch-thick rounds

1½ cups dashi

2 tablespoons soy sauce

1 tablespoon sake

1 tablespoon mirin

Mackerel—always mackerel—is a great choice for a working lunch to discuss the future of aviation. Fish bones definitely have an interesting curvature (and one that could be applied to airplane design), but I recommend triple-checking that all your fish is completely deboned before digging in.

Yield: 2 servings | Prep time: 55 minutes | Cook time: 35 minutes

1. Rinse the mackerel fillets under cold water and pat them dry with a paper towel. Sprinkle salt on the fillets and let the mackerel drain in a colander for 45 minutes to remove the additional water from the fish.

2. While the mackerel is draining, make the soy-braised daikon radish. Place the daikon in a medium pan and add the dashi, soy sauce, and sake. Bring the liquid to a boil over medium heat and simmer for 10 to 15 minutes, until the daikon pieces are tender and slightly brown on the sides.

3. Take the pan off the heat, then add the mirin to the daikon radish. Stir and set aside for 10 minutes.

4. To prepare the mackerel, bring a medium pot of water to a boil and blanch the fillets for 2 to 3 minutes. This process will remove the odor from the mackerel. Remove the fillets using a strainer, drain, and set aside.

5. Place the fillets in a medium nonstick frying pan, skin-side up, over medium heat. Pour the dashi and sake over the fillets. Add the ginger slices and bring to a simmer. Cover the fillets with a drop lid or a smaller lid so fillets are against the bottom of the pan.

6. In a small bowl, combine the sugar and miso. Add 2 tablespoons of the fish stock from the pan to the miso paste and mix until combined. Add the miso mixture back to the pan with the mackerel, and stir.

7. Cover the pan with the lid and continue to simmer, occasionally spooning the miso stock over the fish until the miso stock becomes thick and glossy, about 7 minutes. Take the pan off the heat and set aside to cool slightly.

8. Place each miso-braised mackerel fillet on a plate, spooning the leftover miso sauce onto the fillet. This is to be accompanied with some pickled daikon radish and a small bowl of Morning Miso Soup (page 17).

CHAPTER 3
DINNER

GRANDMA'S HERRING AND PUMPKIN POT PIE

FOR THE PUMPKIN FILLING:

2 tablespoons salted butter

4 cups cubed pumpkin

1 cup water

1 teaspoon salt

black pepper, to taste

1 teaspoon ground cinnamon

½ teaspoon ground nutmeg

¼ cup heavy cream

FOR THE HERRING/FISH FILLING:

1 pound skin-on herring fillets or any other firm white fish of your choice

1 teaspoon premixed fish spice of your choice, such as Old Bay Seasoning or Robertsons Spice for Fish

½ teaspoon dried mixed herbs

2 tablespoons neutral-flavored oil

1 medium yellow onion, diced

1½ cups diced large carrots

3 cloves garlic, diced

1½ cups button mushrooms, sliced

½ cup white wine

3 tablespoons salted butter

3 tablespoons flour

1 cup cream

1 bay leaf

3 sprigs fresh thyme

1 lemon, juiced and zested

salt and pepper, to taste

1 sheet store-bought puff pastry

1 large egg, beaten

4 to 5 black olives, pitted and sliced

Grandma's specialty! It's a bit of work to make, so it wouldn't hurt to ask a young witch for help around the house when making it. Better hurry and get that delivery going before you miss the birthday party!

Yield: 4 to 6 servings | Prep time: 35 minutes | Cook time: 1 hour, 15 minutes

1. To make the pumpkin filling, melt 2 tablespoons of butter in a large pot. Add the cubed pumpkin and sauté for a few minutes, until it has gained some caramelization. Add water and cover the pot with a lid to steam the pumpkin for 5 to 10 minutes.

2. Once the pumpkin has softened, add the teaspoon of salt, crack of black pepper, cinnamon, and nutmeg. Using a masher, mash the pumpkin mixture in the pot until smooth. Add the heavy cream and mix until it is well incorporated. Set aside.

3. Season your herring fillets or other fish fillets with the premixed fish spice and dried mixed herbs. Let the fillets rest for 10 minutes.

4. In a separate nonstick frying pan, add the oil and fry the fish fillets skin-side down. Cook for 1 to 2 minutes until the skin has begun to crisp up. Flip and cook the other side until it is firm. Set aside.

5. To the same frying pan, add the diced onion and carrots, and fry until softened.

6. Add the diced garlic and sliced mushrooms to the pan and sauté until softened and browned.

7. Add the white wine to the pan to deglaze. Add the butter to the same pan and make sure it melts.

8. Add 3 tablespoons of flour to the pan and mix until it forms a roux (a tan-colored thickening agent used for sauce recipes).

9. Add cream to the pan and stir until it is well incorporated and the roux is smooth.

10. Add the bay leaf and fresh thyme to your cream mixture. Let it simmer for 1 minute.

11. Add the cooked herring fillets to the pan and let the mixture simmer for 3 minutes.

12. Add the lemon juice and zest to the mixture. Break the herring fillets into chunks and skim any excess oil from the cream mixture. Add salt and pepper to taste. Discard the bay leaf and sprigs of thyme. Set aside.

ASSEMBLING

1. Preheat your oven to 350°F.

2. In an 8 x 12-inch ovenproof dish, spread an even layer of the pumpkin mixture on the bottom of the dish.

3. Place the fish mixture on top of the pumpkin layer.

4. Cover the mixture with a layer of rolled-out, store-bought puff pastry, 1/4-inch thick, and tuck in the edges.

5. Using some leftover puff pastry, cut out 5 rectangular strips (just over ½ inch in width) and the outline of a fish (including eyes, mouth, fins, and gills).

6. Lay your puff pastry stripes diagonally across the casserole dish. Add the puff pastry fish in the middle of the casserole dish.

7. Brush the top of your puff pastry liberally with a beaten egg and add sliced olives at the end of each puff pastry strip.

8. Bake for 35 to 40 minutes until golden.

9. Serve warm, with a side of fresh garden salad and crusty ciabatta bread.

SECRET MESSAGE FRIED MACKEREL

FOR THE PICKLED CARROTS AND CUCUMBER:

3 medium carrots, julienned

1 small English cucumber, julienned

2 teaspoons coarse kosher salt

¾ cup white vinegar

3⅔ teaspoons sugar

1 whole star anise

1 to 2 dried red chiles

FOR THE FRIED MACKEREL:

3 whole mackerel, gutted and descaled

2 teaspoons premixed fish spice of your choice, such as Old Bay Seasoning or Robertson's Spice for Fish

1 teaspoon fresh thyme

freshly cracked black pepper

4 cups neutral-flavored oil for deep frying

1½ cups flour

2 eggs, lightly beaten

2 cups panko breadcrumbs

1 cup green cabbage, thinly sliced with a mandoline, to serve

1 lemon, sliced into wedges, to serve

sweet chili sauce, to serve

When mackerel is on sale, why not fry it up? It's a nice and comforting dinner to enjoy while you ruminate on the mysterious school newspaper message about a girl who raises flags. Who could it be from?

Yield: 3 servings | Prep time: 35 minutes plus 30 minutes to marinate | Cook time: 21 minutes

1. To make the pickled carrots and cucumber, place the vegetables in a large bowl with the salt. Let them marinate for 10 minutes. This will draw out the moisture and make the vegetables crunchier. Drain well and pat them dry with a kitchen towel.

2. In a separate bowl, combine the vinegar, sugar, star anise, and red chiles. Mix until the sugar has dissolved. Pour the vinegar mixture over the vegetables, cover, and chill in the refrigerator for 30 minutes or overnight.

3. To butterfly your mackerel, use the tip of a sharp knife to slice underneath the fin and make a cut underneath the belly all the way to the tail (use the spine as a guide and make sure not to break any other areas of the skin). Flip the fish and repeat the process on the other side. Use a pair of scissors to cut down through the backbone behind the head and in front of the tail. Carefully separate the bones from the flesh. Discard the head and trim the fins. The mackerel tail should remain intact. Use a pair of tweezers if there are any remaining fish bones in the fillets. Repeat for the rest of the mackerel. Lightly season the mackerel on both sides with the premixed fish spice, thyme, and pepper.

4. Add the oil to a wok or deep frying pan over medium-high heat. Heat until the oil reaches 350°F.

5. Place the flour, eggs, and panko breadcrumbs in separate large bowls and dredge the butterflied fish in each ingredient, respectively.

6. Fry the fish for 5 to 7 minutes, flipping it halfway through the cooking time or until it turns golden brown. Place the first cooked fillet on a wire rack while you fry the rest.

7. On each of 3 plates, serve one fried mackerel with the shredded cabbage, pickled vegetables, lemon wedges, and sweet chili sauce.

TIP: *If you cannot find mackerel, large sardines are a great alternative. To debone a sardine, run your fingers parallel to the bones on either side. Gently crack the spine by the head and tail. Get a good grip of the spine and gently pull away from the body. Cut off the head and trim the fins with a sharp knife or scissors.*

DATE NIGHT PAN-SEARED SALMON IN BEURRE BLANC SAUCE

FOR THE HONEY-ROASTED CARROTS:

4 tablespoons salted butter

1 tablespoon minced garlic

2 cups baby carrots

2 tablespoons honey

Bring home a taste of the Adriatic Sea on date night with this French-inspired dish! Seared salmon fillet served in a creamy *beurre blanc* sauce with honey-roasted carrots will surely make your special someone pig out. Warning: please do not operate any aircrafts or similar machinery while enjoying this meal.

Yield: 2 servings | Prep time: 7 minutes | Cook time: 45 minutes

1. To make the garlic and honey roasted carrots, melt the butter in a nonstick frying pan over medium heat.

2. Add the garlic and sauté until it is aromatic, about 1 minute. Add the carrots and honey and sauté for an additional 2 minutes.

3. Transfer the carrots to a roasting pan and roast for 10 minutes at 350°F.

FOR THE BEURRE BLANC SAUCE:
½ cup dry white wine (sauvignon blanc and chardonnay are great options)

2 tablespoons shallots or white onion, minced

3 tablespoons heavy cream

juice and zest of ½ lemon

½ cup salted butter, chilled and cubed

dash of salt, ground cayenne pepper or paprika

FOR THE SALMON:
2 (7-ounce) fresh Norwegian skin-on salmon fillets, pin bones removed

salt and pepper, to taste

4 tablespoons neutral-flavored oil, divided

4. To make the beurre blanc sauce, add the white wine and shallots or white onion to a saucepan over medium heat. Let the mixture simmer until 2 to 3 tablespoons of wine are left in the saucepan, 10 to 15 minutes.

5. Add the heavy cream, lemon juice, and lemon zest to the wine mixture, and whisk. Turn your stove down to medium-low heat.

6. Add the cubes of butter one at a time, whisking constantly until the sauce has emulsified (or until it is creamy and thick).

7. Place a strainer on top of a bowl and separate the shallots or onions from the beurre blanc sauce. Finally, season the sauce with salt and ground cayenne or paprika, to taste.

8. Season your salmon fillets with salt and pepper on both sides.

9. Add 2 tablespoons of oil to a large nonstick frying pan over medium-high heat and place the two salmon fillets skin-side down. Let the skin crisp up, then flip to cook the other side. Both sides of the salmon should be golden brown. Place the salmon fillets in a roasting pan and let them cook in the oven for 6 to 8 minutes, depending how thick the salmon fillets are.

10. To serve, drizzle the beurre blanc sauce over the crispy salmon and serve with the honey-roasted carrots. This dish will be even better with a glass of white wine!

TIP: *Beurre blanc is a French white butter sauce that pairs really well with any type of seafood, as well as chicken or vegetables. If your beurre blanc sauce begins to separate, take the saucepan off the heat and allow the beurre blanc to cool to 110°F. Add 1 tablespoon of cold water or cream and place it back on the stove over low heat, whisking thoroughly until it becomes pale, thick, and creamy again.*

TIP: *Another great addition to beurre blanc sauce is fresh chopped chives or parsley.*

CHORIZO SPAGHETTI BOLOGNESE

1½ tablespoons olive oil

¼ pound smoked chorizo sausage, cubed

2 medium yellow onions, finely diced

2 carrots, diced

2 celery sticks, finely diced

2 baby leeks, diced

2 cloves garlic, finely minced

2 to 3 sprigs rosemary, leaves picked and finely chopped

2 pounds ground beef

2 (14.1-ounce) cans plum tomatoes

½ cup red wine

2 tablespoons tomato paste

¼ cup finely chopped fresh basil

1 teaspoon dried oregano

If pigs could fly, they would have this Spanish-Italian spaghetti Bolognese every day. Buon appetito!

Yield: 6 to 8 servings | Prep time: 15 minutes | Cook time: 1 hour, 30 minutes

1. Heat the oil in a nonstick deep frying pan over medium-high heat. Add the chopped chorizo sausage and sauté for 2 to 3 minutes, or until the oil turns a red color and becomes fragrant.

2. Add the onions, carrots, celery, baby leeks, garlic, and rosemary to the pan and fry for an additional 7 to 10 minutes, or until the vegetables have softened and the onions become translucent. Set the vegetables aside in a separate bowl.

3. Increase the heat to high and add the ground beef. Cook for 5 minutes, until the meat has browned.

2 bay leaves

1 teaspoon smoked paprika

1 beef stock cube

1 red chile, deseeded and finely chopped

6 cherry tomatoes, sliced in half

1 tablespoon Worcestershire sauce

salt and pepper, to taste

1 (16-ounce) package spaghetti

2 tablespoons brown sugar

⅓ cup parmesan, for serving

torn fresh basil, crusty bread, and red wine, for serving

4. Return the cooked vegetables to the pan. Add the tomatoes, red wine, tomato paste, basil, oregano, bay leaves, smoked paprika, beef stock cube, chile, halved cherry tomatoes, Worcestershire sauce, salt, and pepper into the pan. Mix well, making sure to break up the tomatoes with your spoon. Decrease the heat to medium and gently simmer for 1 hour and 15 minutes, stirring occasionally until you have a rich and thick sauce.

5. Before the Bolognese sauce is finished (around the 1-hour mark), cook the spaghetti according to the package instructions. When you are boiling the pasta, add a bit of salt and oil to the water and make sure that the pasta is al dente. Once cooked, drain the spaghetti, reserving ½ cup of the cooking water.

6. Before the Bolognese sauce is fully cooked (5 minutes before the end of cooking time), add the brown sugar and season to taste. Cook for another 5 minutes. If the sauce is too thick, you can thin it down a bit with the pasta water. Add the spaghetti to the Bolognese sauce and toss so the sauce coats all the pasta.

7. Serve the Chorizo Spaghetti Bolognese with a generous sprinkling of parmesan and torn fresh basil. This is great with crusty ciabatta bread and a glass of red wine.

TIP: *The longer cooking time for this Bolognese sauce is worth it, as the flavors develop. I do suggest making a big batch and storing it in the freezer to have on hand when you've had a hectic day fixing planes and stopping the villains.*

TIP: *To make this kid friendly, replace the red wine with a good-quality beef stock.*

TIP: *Use a pan with a wide surface area so your ground beef can brown faster. If you do not have a large pan, I suggest dividing your beef in half and cooking it in intervals.*

CHICKEN CONGEE (OKAYU)

2 cups jasmine rice

1 tablespoon vegetable oil

½ teaspoon salt, plus more as needed

3 quarts water

3 to 4 dried scallops, roughly chopped

1 inch knob ginger, sliced

3 green onions, chopped

2 pounds bone-in chicken thighs and breasts, cut into pieces

1 tablespoon soy sauce

1 tablespoon cornstarch or flour

1 teaspoon sugar

1 tablespoon sesame oil

additional chopped green onions, soy sauce, and toasted sesame seeds, for garnishing (optional)

Congee is a delicious rice porridge that will help you get your strength back after fighting demons. It's easy to make, especially if you need a quick and filling meal while on a long journey to break a curse and finding the Great Forest Spirit. Share with new friends, but be wary of opportunistic monks!

Yield: 5 to 7 servings | Prep time: 45 minutes | Cook time: 1 hour, 20 minutes

1. Combine the rice, oil, and salt in a large bowl and let the mixture sit for 30 minutes.

2. To a large, heavy-bottomed pot over high heat, add the water and bring to a boil.

3. Add the oil-rice mixture, dried scallops, ginger, green onions (reserve a bit for garnishing), and chicken pieces.

4. Bring the contents of the pot to a boil again, then immediately turn down the heat to medium low. Allow the congee to simmer, covered, for 1 to 1¼ hours, or until the rice starts to break apart. Make sure to stir the congee occasionally so it does not burn at the bottom.

5. After the chicken has cooked, move the chicken pieces to a bowl and allow them to cool. Shred the chicken and remove the bones. Season the shredded chicken with soy sauce, cornstarch or flour, sugar, and sesame oil. Mix well.

6. Add the shredded chicken back into the congee. Bring the heat up to a boil and cook for an additional 5 minutes (so the cornstarch is fully cooked). Season with salt to taste.

7. Serve the congee in individual bowls and garnish with green onions, soy sauce, and toasted sesame seeds, if desired.

TIP: *Other great garnishes that go with congee include chile oil, fried shallots, and chopped fresh cilantro. I also like to add a tablespoon of cornflakes for some extra crunch.*

HEARTY BEEF STEW TO FEED A CROWD

2 pounds stewing beef or beef chuck, cubed into 1½-inch chunks

1½ teaspoons salt

1 teaspoon black pepper

6 tablespoons flour

2 tablespoons neutral-flavored vegetable oil, or more if needed

1 medium yellow onion, diced

2 to 3 medium carrots, diced

2 stalks celery, chopped

4 cloves garlic, minced

¼ cup tomato paste

2 large potatoes, cut into 1-inch chunks

2 cups beef broth

1 bay leaf

2 teaspoons smoked paprika

2 teaspoons fresh thyme sprigs

2 tablespoons Worcestershire sauce

1½ teaspoons sugar

½ cup red wine

chopped fresh parsley, for garnishing

rice or ciabatta, to serve

salt and pepper, to taste

This hearty beef stew tastes even better in the sky with your pirate family. This meal is great to feed a crowd or an entire pirate crew, although you'll definitely get better reviews if you've managed to get everyone to fall in love with you first!

Yield: 6 to 8 servings | Prep time: 15 minutes | Cook time: 1 hour, 10 minutes

1. Season the beef with salt and pepper in a large bowl. Toss in the flour, coating the beef on all sides.

2. Heat the vegetable oil in a large, heavy-bottomed pot over medium heat. Working in batches to avoid overcrowding the pot, fry the beef until it has browned on all sides. This should take about 3 to 5 minutes per batch; add 1 tablespoon more of oil for each batch. Transfer the beef to a separate bowl and set aside.

3. Using the same pot, fry the onions, carrots, and celery until they have softened. Add the garlic and tomato paste. Stirring constantly, cook until the vegetables are fragrant and the tomato paste has become dark.

4. Add the potatoes, beef broth, bay leaf, smoked paprika, sprigs of thyme, Worcestershire sauce, sugar, and red wine. Using a wooden spoon, make sure to scrape off the browned bits at the bottom of the pot.

5. Lower the heat and bring the stew to a boil. Return the beef with its juices back to the pot. Cover with a lid and let simmer for 45 minutes to 1 hour, depending on the cut of beef or until the beef is tender. You may need to add more water to the stew during the cooking time if you find the stew is getting a bit too thick.

6. Season the stew with salt and pepper to taste. Remove the bay leaf and sprigs of thyme, and garnish with chopped fresh parsley.

7. Serve warm with fluffy rice or crusty ciabatta.

JAPANESE CREAM STEW

½ pound chicken breasts, cubed into 1½-inch chunks

salt and pepper, to taste

1 head broccoli, cut into small florets

1 tablespoon neutral-flavored vegetable oil

1 tablespoon salted butter

1 medium yellow onion, quartered and layers separated

1 large potato, cut into 1-inch chunks

2 to 3 medium carrots, cut diagonally into bite-size pieces

1 stalk celery, sliced

2 cups chicken or vegetable broth

2 bay leaves

8 button mushrooms, thinly sliced

⅓ cup green peas

FOR THE BÉCHAMEL SAUCE:
3 tablespoons salted butter

5 tablespoons flour

1 cup whole milk

salt and pepper, to taste

¼ teaspoon ground nutmeg

steamed rice, for serving

fresh parsley, for garnishing

Japanese Cream Stew, also known as "White Stew," is rich and creamy. This is a must-have after your first "borrowing" mission to get some sugar and tissue for your mom. Just make sure you are not caught by any of the giant house residents, including that nosy housemaid or pest control for that matter!

Yield: 2 to 3 servings | Prep time: 20 minutes | Cook time: 40 minutes

1. Season the chicken with salt and pepper, and set aside.

2. In a medium pot over medium heat, boil the broccoli florets for 2 minutes, until they are tender. Immediately shock the broccoli by placing the florets in a bowl of ice water for 2 minutes to retain their green color. Drain and set aside to cool.

3. Heat the vegetable oil and butter in a large, heavy pot over medium heat. Add the diced chicken to the pot and fry the chicken until it has browned on all sides, for about 7 minutes.

4. Add the onion to the pot and sauté until softened, for another 7 minutes.

5. Add the potato, carrots, and celery and sauté for 2 minutes.

6. Add enough chicken or vegetable broth to cover the majority of the vegetables. Add the bay leaves and bring the stew to a boil, then cover and reduce the heat to a simmer. Cook for 8 minutes.

7. While the cream stew is cooking, start the béchamel sauce. In a small pot, melt the butter on medium heat. Make a roux by adding the flour, and continuously whisk until it is well incorporated, 4 to 7 minutes. (The roux should bubble.)

8. Warm the milk in the microwave for 30 seconds to 1 minute. While continuously stirring, slowly add the warm milk to the pot until the béchamel sauce becomes thick and creamy.

9. Season the sauce with salt, pepper, and nutmeg. Stir well, then set aside.

10. Uncover the stewpot and check the potatoes. The potatoes are fully cooked when you can insert a fork into them with ease.

11. Ladle about ½ cup of broth into the béchamel sauce and stir until combined. Pour the béchamel sauce into the stewpot and gently stir without breaking apart any of the vegetables.

12. Add the sliced mushrooms, cooked broccoli, and green peas. Simmer for an additional 3 to 5 minutes on low heat, uncovered. Season the stew with salt and pepper, to taste.

13. Serve the stew with steamed rice and garnish with chopped parsley.

TIP: *Pour small amounts of warm milk into the roux when making your béchamel sauce to keep lumps from forming. Add ½ teaspoon garlic powder to the béchamel sauce when adding the salt, pepper, and nutmeg to the sauce for stronger flavor.*

CRYSTAL SKIN TAIWANESE DUMPLING (BA WAN)

FOR THE GROUND PORK FILLING:

6 dried shiitake mushrooms

2 tablespoons dried baby shrimp

8 ounces ground pork

3 tablespoons soy sauce, plus more to serve

½ teaspoon salt

1 tablespoon sugar

1 teaspoon Chinese five-spice powder

½ teaspoon ground white pepper

¼ cup bamboo shoots

2 tablespoons neutral-flavored oil

3 cloves garlic, minced

2 tablespoons shallots or green onions, chopped

1 tablespoon oyster sauce

1 tablespoon Shaoxing rice wine vinegar

½ teaspoon toasted sesame oil, plus more to serve

FOR THE CRYSTAL SKIN DUMPLING WRAPPERS:

½ cup tapioca starch

1 cup wheat starch

½ teaspoon vegetable oil

½ teaspoon salt

¾ cup boiling water

4 cups water, for steaming

cilantro, for garnishing

toasted sesame seed oil, for serving

soy sauce, for serving

You may remember a suspicious food stall that served stomach of coelacanth (a fish from the dinosaur period). Let's stick to this delicious dumpling instead. *Ba wan* is a popular Taiwanese street food similar to a large stuffed dumpling. Traditionally, ba wan is made of tapioca starch and wheat starch and stuffed with pork, bamboo shoots, and shiitake mushrooms. However, this is a fusion between ba wan and the Chinese *har gow*, or crystal skin shrimp dumplings.

Yield: 2 giant dumplings | Prep time: 1 hour 15 minutes | Cook time: 45 minutes

1. Place the dried shiitake mushrooms and dried shrimp in a bowl of boiling water and let them steep for 20 minutes. Once they are soft, dice and set aside. Reserve 4 to 5 tablespoons of the soaking water. This is packed with umami flavor.

2. In a separate bowl, season the ground pork with the soy sauce, salt, sugar, five-spice powder, and ground white pepper. Using a pair of chopsticks, mix clockwise until all the ingredients are combined.

3. Add in the diced mushrooms, shrimp, and bamboo shoots. Place the pork mixture in the fridge and let it chill for 30 minutes.

4. Heat the oil in a large cast-iron pan over medium heat.

5. Fry the garlic cloves and shallots or green onions for 1 minutes, or until they are slightly crispy and fragrant. Add the seasoned ground pork and sauté for 8 minutes until all sides are browned.

6. Add in the oyster sauce, Shaoxing rice wine vinegar, sesame oil, and a few tablespoons of the shiitake-shrimp water to the pork. Stir fry for 2 to 5 minutes until the sauce thickens and the pork is fully cooked. Season to taste and set side.

7. To prepare your crystal skin wrapper dough, combine the tapioca starch, wheat starch, oil, salt, and boiling water. The water quantity may differ, depending on the quality and type of wheat starch you are using. Most chefs base the amount of water they use on how the dough feels, which should be enough to form a soft and smooth, malleable dough. (See the tip box for more information.) If the dough cracks when you roll it out, it means you need to increase the quantity of boiling water. Once it has reached the right consistency, let the dough relax for 5 minutes.

8. Reserve one quarter of the dough and set aside. Divide the remaining dough into 2 large balls and roll the one dough ball as thin as you possibly can between 2 plastic sheets or silicone baking mats. Place 2 to 3 tablespoons of the pork mixture in the center and fold over the edges with the help of your silicone mat. Pinch the sides and place it on a heat-proof glassware or dish. Repeat for the other large dough ball. Place the plate of dumplings in a bamboo steamer.

9. For decoration, take the reserved small ball of dough and roll it out into 6 small teardrop shapes. Place 3 teardrops on top of your ba wan (using a bit of water as glue) and set aside. Repeat for the other dumpling.

10. In a wok, bring 4 cups of water to a boil over high heat, then reduce the heat so it maintains a gentle simmer. Place the bamboo steamer on top of the wok, making sure that the bottom of the steamer does not touch the water. Steam for 25 to 35 minutes until the skin becomes translucent.

11. Serve each dumpling hot on a separate plate with chopped cilantro, toasted sesame oil, and soy sauce.

TIP: *When making the crystal skin dumpling wrappers, it is essential to use boiling water. Here are a few suggestions to get the right feel of dough.*

TIP: *The dough is too dry when:*

- *It is difficult to roll out paper thin.*
- *The dough cracks on the side when rolled out into a circle.*
- *It tears easily when wrapping around the filling.*

TIP: *The dough is too wet when:*

- *It is sticky and difficult to roll out.*

TIP: *Add a small amount of wheat starch to the dough if it is too wet, or add boiling water if it is too dry. Knead the mixture again until it is smooth and even, and repeat. Remember to let the dough relax for 5 minutes.*

CHAPTER 4
SNACKS AND STREET FOOD

CLASSIC TEMPURA SELECTION

FOR THE TEMPURA FILLING:

1 cup tiger shrimp, peeled and deveined, tails on

½ cup green beans, trimmed

1 medium eggplant, sliced into ¼-inch-thick rounds

1 red bell pepper, julienned

FOR THE TERIYAKI DIPPING SAUCE:

2 tablespoons mirin

4 tablespoons soy sauce

1 teaspoon brown sugar

2 tablespoons sake (optional)

¼ teaspoon toasted sesame oil

¼ teaspoon toasted sesame seeds

FOR THE WASABI SOY DIPPING SAUCE:

½ teaspoon wasabi

2 tablespoons mirin

2 tablespoons soy sauce

½ teaspoon brown sugar

FOR THE TEMPURA BATTER:

1 cup flour

¼ cup cornstarch, plus extra for dusting

1 large egg

1 cup chilled soda or other neutral-flavored sparkling water

4 to 6 ice cubes

neutral-flavored oil, for shallow frying

kosher salt, to taste

½ lemon, cut into slices, for serving

No one can resist a super-crispy selection of tempura goodies in the streets of the Spirit Realm. You can use a wide range of fresh ingredients, but the most popular options include seafood (shrimp, calamari heads, scallops, slices of whitefish), root vegetables (sweet potato, lotus root, onion) and mushrooms. The recipe below has my favorite meat-and-vegetable selection.

Yield: 3 to 4 servings | Prep time: 12 minutes | Cook time: 20 minutes

1. Score deep cuts underneath each shrimp (about halfway through the shrimp but not cutting all the way through) as this will prevent them from curling when frying.

2. Combine all the ingredients for the teriyaki dipping sauce into a bowl and mix until the sugar has dissolved. Set aside.

3. In a separate bowl, mix all the wasabi soy dipping sauce ingredients. Set aside.

4. To make the tempura batter, mix the flour and cornstarch in a bowl until well combined.

5. Make a well in the center, and crack your egg into it. Add the soda or sparkling water to the well. Using a pair of chopsticks, stir the mixture until the batter is just combined but still lumpy.

6. Add the ice cubes to the batter and place it in the fridge to chill for at least 5 minutes.

7. Heat your oil in a heavy pot or wok.

8. Lightly dust your shrimp and assortment of vegetables in a bit of cornstarch.

9. Once the oil has reached a temperature of 350°F, gently dip your shrimp and vegetables in the chilled tempura batter and place them in the oil. Fry until a crispy outer shell forms around the ingredients and the shrimp has turned pink. This should take 2 minutes. Try not to overcrowd the pot or wok, and fry in batches. For an extra-crispy shell, add 1 to 2 tablespoons of tempura batter on top of the tempura prawns and vegetables while frying.

10. Place the tempura on a wire rack and, while it is still hot, sprinkle it with kosher salt to taste.

11. Serve immediately on a large platter with the 2 dipping sauces in mini sauce dishes and slices of lemon around the tempura, then dig in. The tempura is also great with some fried shrimp-flavored chips, which can be found at your local Asian grocery store. You can fry these in the same oil as your tempura.

TIP: *Serve your tempura immediately as it loses its crispiness the longer it stands out.*

TIP: *Pick up any crumbs left in the oil and save them; these crumbs are called* tenkasu. *They are a great addition to okonomiyaki (page 72) and takoyaki (page 63).*

TIP: *Using a pair of chopsticks to mix your tempura batter prevents overmixing.*

TIP: *For another great flavor combination, lightly dust your tempura with your favorite curry powder after frying.*

TEN-DON (TEMPURA RICE BOWL)

INGREDIENTS FOR TEMPURA:
tempura batter (page 52)

3 tiger prawns, shelled and deveined, tails on

6 green beans, trimmed

1 red bell pepper, julienned

1 large soft-boiled egg, peeled

1 nori sheet, cut into 5-inch squares

kosher salt, to taste

1 large bowl cooked jasmine rice

FOR THE TENTSUYU SAUCE:
1 cup dashi stock

¼ cup soy sauce

¼ cup mirin

1 tablespoon brown sugar

grated daikon (optional)

A selection of golden crispy shrimp, egg, *nori*, and vegetable tempura served over steamy rice and drizzled with *tentsuyu* dipping sauce. A dish that's hearty enough to keep you going, whether you're an overworked six-armed bathhouse spirit or have just had a long day.

Yield: 1 serving | Prep time: 10 minutes | Cook time: 25 minutes

1. Make the tempura batter.

2. Fry the prawns, green beans, and bell pepper in the tempura batter by following the steps in the Classic Tempura Selection recipe on page 52.

3. Fry the soft-boiled egg dipped in tempura batter for 1 to 2 minutes maximum to retain that runny yolk. The nori squares require a delicate hand, so dip them in and out of the batter as quickly as possible and immediately place them in the hot oil for frying. Cook for a few seconds and immediately drain on a rack once the nori has turned crispy. While the tempura is still hot, sprinkle it with kosher salt to taste.

4. To make the tentsuyu sauce, combine all the ingredients in a small pot. Place the pot over medium heat and simmer for a few minutes or until the sugar has completely dissolved. Take the pot off the heat and let the sauce cool slightly. Add grated daikon, if desired, and serve warm.

5. Prepare the tempura bowl by packing freshly cooked jasmine rice in a bowl. Place the hot tempura over the rice in a circular shape. Finally, drizzle the sauce over the tempura and serve hot.

TIP: *If you are using leftover tempura from the previous day, reheat it in the oven or in the air fryer for 5 minutes, or until warm, to retain the crispiness of the batter.*

TRIO OF ONIGIRI

FOR THE CHAR SIU FILLING:

¼ cup hoisin sauce

⅓ cup brown sugar

⅓ cup Shaoxing rice wine vinegar

⅓ cup plus 2 tablespoons syrup or honey

1 teaspoon salt

2 tablespoons dark soy sauce

1½ tablespoons oyster sauce

1 teaspoon Chinese five-spice powder

3 to 4 cloves garlic, minced

1 teaspoon sesame oil

1 block red bean curd

2 to 3 drops red food coloring

2½ pounds pork loin or neck, cut into 3 long pieces

salt and pepper, to taste

FOR THE SPICY TUNA MAYO FILLING:

6 ounces canned tuna, drained

¼ teaspoon togarashi

¼ cup Kewpie Mayonnaise

1 green onion, finely sliced

2 tablespoons combination of black and white sesame seeds

FOR THE UMEBOSHI FILLING:

1 Japanese umeboshi, pitted

FOR THE ONIGIRI:

2½ cups of cooked jasmine rice

1 teaspoon salt, to taste

1 nori sheet, cut into 2-inch strips

Whether you're trapped in the realm of spirits or your parents have just turned into pigs, this is the go-to snack for regaining your strength. *Onigiri* is very versatile and can be adapted to your favorite flavor combinations. This is also a great way to use leftover or pantry ingredients. You can choose between a sweet and savory Chinese-style roasted pork filling, spicy tuna mayo, or the classic pickled plum filling. You'll surely be able to handle anything if you eat all three!

Yield: 3 to 4 servings | Prep time: 22 minutes, plus 8 hours to marinate | Cook time: 40 minutes

1. To make the char siu, combine all the ingredients (except the pork) in a large bowl and mix until well combined. Place the pork in the marinade, ensuring that it is fully submerged. Let it rest in the fridge for 8 hours or overnight.

2. Preheat the oven to 400°F. Pour boiling water into the bottom of the roasting pan and place a rack on top. Place the pork on the rack where it is not in direct contact with the water, and roast for 20 minutes.

3. Pour the remaining marinade into a small pot over medium heat. Bring the marinade to a boil and simmer for 5 minutes, until the sauce has slightly thickened. Divide the marinade between 2 bowls—1 will be used for basting and the other for serving.

4. Remove the pork from the oven and baste both sides with the cooked marinade. Return to the oven and roast for 10 more minutes. Drizzle a small amount of honey (around 2 tablespoons) over the pork and roast until the honey starts to caramelize, about 2 to 5 minutes.

5. Remove the pork from the oven and let it rest for 10 minutes before slicing. Dice it into bite-size pieces and set it aside. You will have leftover char siu, which goes amazingly well with ramen or just plain rice.

6. For the spicy tuna mayo filling, combine all the ingredients in a medium bowl, mix, and set aside.

7. In a large bowl, season the cooked jasmine rice with salt and mix until it is well incorporated. Use a rice paddle to keep from breaking up the rice too.

8. Dip your hands in a bowl of water to help prevent the rice from sticking. Roll roughly ½ cup of rice into a ball. Gently flatten it while creating a well in the center. Add 1 tablespoon of the char siu filling and ½ teaspoon of the marinade to the center of the rice.

9. Using your hands, mold the rice around the well to cover the filling completely, then gently shape the rice ball into a wide triangular shape using the palm of your hands, rotating the rice ball as you go. Try not to squeeze the rice too hard, as you do not want the rice to break up. Finally, place a strip of nori underneath the onigiri (shiny side facing toward you) and fold it up toward the middle of the onigiri. Set aside.

10. Repeat the same onigiri shaping technique with the rest of the fillings. For the spicy tuna onigiri, use 1 tablespoon of the tuna filling. You may also roll the sides of the onigiri in a mixture of black and white sesame seeds, and wrap a strip of nori underneath. For the umeboshi onigiri, I tried to stick close to the original film when Chihiro was encouraged to eat the onigiri to regain her strength. This onigiri is left plain with 1 umeboshi as the filling.

11. Serve warm or at room temperature.

TIP: *If you are uncomfortable shaping the onigiri with your hands, I recommend placing some plastic wrap on a table and place 2 to 3 tablespoons of rice on the plastic wrap. Add 1 tablespoon of your desired filling in the middle of the rice bed and add an additional 2 to 3 tablespoons of rice on top, completely covering the filling. Lift the edges of the plastic wrap toward the middle while forming a rice ball. Gently shape the rice ball into a triangle using your hands. Take the plastic wrap off and set the onigiri aside. Repeat for the rest.*

TIP: *Cover the onigiri as the rice tends to get hard when exposed to air.*

TIP: *Other great flavor combinations include grilled salmon, leftover rotisserie chicken with a lemon sauce, kimchi with spam, bonito flakes, prawns with mayo, or sautéed shiitake mushrooms. The list is endless.*

MENCHI KATSU

1 medium onion, finely diced

2 tablespoons neutral-flavored oil

1 green onion, finely diced

1 clove garlic, finely diced

1 pound ground beef

5 tablespoons panko breadcrumbs

1½ tablespoons soy sauce

1 large egg, lightly beaten

1 teaspoon salt

½ teaspoon freshly cracked black pepper

½ teaspoon nutmeg

1 tablespoon ketchup or tomato sauce

1 teaspoon Worcestershire sauce

finely shredded green cabbage, for serving

There are many different types of *katsu* (pork, chicken, and even cheese), but menchi katsu is made of flavorful fried ground beef. This delicious, deep-fried snack is the perfect pick-me-up after a bike ride to the market.

Yield: 6 servings | Prep time: 20 minutes | Cook time: 35 minutes

1. Sauté the onion over medium heat with a bit of oil until it has become golden brown and translucent. Add the green onion and garlic and sauté for a few seconds, until aromatic. Transfer the onion mixture to a large bowl and set aside to cool.

2. To the same bowl, add the ground beef, panko breadcrumbs, soy sauce, egg, salt, pepper, nutmeg, ketchup or tomato sauce, and Worcestershire sauce.

3. Using clean hands, combine the beef mixture until it becomes pale and sticky. Roughly divide the mixture into 6 balls.

FOR COATING THE MENCHI KATSU:

½ cup all-purpose flour

2 large eggs, lightly beaten

1 cup panko breadcrumbs

neutral-flavored oil, for deep frying

FOR THE MENCHI TONKATSU SAUCE:

1 tablespoon Worcestershire sauce

1 tablespoon ketchup/tomato sauce

1 tablespoon hot water

1 tablespoon sweet chilli sauce

1 teaspoon lemon juice

4. Repeatedly toss each ball from one hand to the other repeatedly to release any air pockets, then shape them into oval patties and let rest in the refrigerator while setting up your dredging station.

5. To set up your dredging station, prepare 3 bowls that contain flour, beaten eggs, and panko breadcrumbs, respectively. Start by coating your first patty in the flour, dipping it in the egg mixture, then coating it in panko breadcrumbs. Repeat for the rest of the patties and set aside.

6. Add oil to a wok or deep frying pan over medium-high heat. Heat until the oil reaches 350°F.

7. Gently place the patties into the oil and fry for 3 minutes on each side (a total of 6 minutes). Fry your patties in small batches so that the wok is not overcrowded. Place the patties onto a wire rack so that air can circulate at the bottom of the patties.

8. To make the Menchi Tonkatsu sauce, combine all the ingredients in a bowl until no lumps remain.

9. Serve the menchi katsu on a platter while hot, with the menchi tonkatsu sauce and finely shredded cabbage on the side. Alternatively, wrap each menchi katsu with a sheet of wax paper (the top half of the menchi katsu should be exposed) and take it as a on-the-go snack.

TIP: *For some extra-cheesy goodness, add a cube of mozzarella cheese to the center of your Menchi Katsu when you are shaping the patties.*

SMOKY AND SWEET YAKITORI

½ cup soy sauce

4 tablespoons mirin

2 tablespoons sake

2 tablespoons brown sugar

3 tablespoons water

2 tablespoons neutral-flavored oil, divided

1 tablespoon toasted sesame oil

½ teaspoon grated ginger

1 pound boneless skin-on chicken thighs, cut into bite-size pieces

6 to 8 (6-inch) bamboo or metal skewers

1 large green onion, cut into 1-inch batons

Glazed in a homemade *yakitori* sauce, these tempting homemade Japanese savory-sweet chicken and green onion skewers are hard to resist! A crowd-pleaser, especially during a family barbecue. Better watch out for those magical raccoon dogs that may steal a piece while trying to fit into human society!

Yield: 3 to 4 servings | Prep time: 10 minutes, 1 to 2 hours or overnight to marinate | Cook time: 40 minutes

1. In a medium bowl, whisk together the soy sauce, mirin, sake, brown sugar, water, 1 tablespoon of neutral-flavored oil, toasted sesame oil, and ginger.

2. Add the chicken pieces to the marinade and let them rest for 1 to 2 hours or overnight.

3. If using bamboo skewers, soak the skewers in water for 10 to 15 minutes. This will prevent them from burning while roasting at a later stage.

1 medium green pepper, julienned

salt and pepper, to taste

toasted sesame seeds

togarashi and lemon wedges, for garnishing

4. Thread the marinated chicken pieces on the skewers, alternating between the chicken, green onion batons, and green pepper. Season with salt and pepper on both sides.

5. Drizzle both sides of the skewers with 1 tablespoon of neutral-flavored oil to prevent sticking when cooking. Place the chicken skewers on a baking sheet lined with foil.

6. In a small pot over medium to high heat, add the leftover marinade and bring it to a boil. When it boils, reduce the heat to low and simmer, uncovered, until the sauce has reduced by half or becomes thick and glossy, 12 to 20 minutes. Set aside and let it cool to room temperature. Note that the sauce will thicken even further as it cools.

7. Preheat the broiler over medium-high heat at 350°F. Alternatively, you can grill these on your barbecue. Once the oven is hot, broil the skewers for 6 minutes. Baste both sides of the skewer and flip. Continue to broil for 3 to 4 minutes on the other side, or until the sauce begins to caramelize (10 minutes).

8. Transfer the skewers to a serving plate, sprinkle them with toasted sesame seeds, and brush the sauce over them 1 last time. Serve hot with a generous sprinkle of togarashi and lemon wedges.

TIP: *Keep an eye on your yakitori when cooking them, as they have a tendency to burn due to the sugar in the sauce.*

TIP: *Crowd the skewers to prevent your chicken from drying out.*

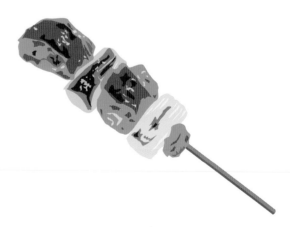

TAKOYAKI

FOR BOILING THE OCTOPUS:
¼ pound fresh octopus

4 cloves

2 bay leaves

1 tablespoon lemon zest

FOR THE TAKOYAKI BATTER:
¾ cup all-purpose flour

¼ cup rice flour

2 teaspoons baking powder

½ teaspoon salt

2 large eggs

1 teaspoon soy sauce

1½ cups dashi stock

4 green onions, thinly sliced, divided

½ cup fried tenkasu, or tempura scraps (see the Classic Tempura Selection tip on page 53)

1 tablespoon *beni shoga*, or pickled red ginger, minced

4 cups neutral-flavored oil, for shallow frying

2 tablespoons Kewpie Mayonnaise

¼ cup bonito flakes

1 sheet nori, shredded

FOR THE TAKOYAKI SAUCE:
2 tablespoons sugar

2 tablespoons tomato sauce or ketchup

1 tablespoon Worcestershire sauce

1 tablespoon soy sauce

1 tablespoon oyster sauce

Takoyaki, or octopus balls, are a super-popular and delicious Japanese street food—no doubt something you would find among the mysterious stalls and street vendors of the Spirit Realm. If you happen to have a *takoyaki* pan, feel free to use it. However, this recipe uses half-sphere silicone molds, which you can buy at any baking shop.

Yield: 1 serving | Prep time: 20 minutes, 1 hour, 10 minutes for chilling | Cook time: 1 hour, 20 minutes

1. To prepare the octopus, place the octopus, cloves, bay leaves, and lemon zest in a large pot filled with enough cold water to cover the octopus. Bring the water to a boil over high heat, then lower the heat to medium low and let it simmer for 1 hour and 15 minutes. The time may vary depending on the weight and thickness of the octopus, but when a knife can slide with ease into the largest part of a leg, it is cooked thoroughly. Take the octopus out of the water and let the octopus cool completely, then cut the meat into bite-size pieces.

2. To make the takoyaki batter, whisk the all-purpose flour, rice flour, baking powder, and salt in a large mixing bowl.

3. Make a well in the center of the flour mixture and add the eggs, soy sauce, and dashi stock. Whisk until well incorporated.

4. Reserve 1 tablespoon of the green onion (green parts only), then fold the remainder of the green onions with the tenkasu and pickled red ginger into the batter. Transfer the batter into a measuring cup with a spout for easy pouring.

5. Fill 1½ inch half-sphere silicone molds ¾ full with batter, and add the octopus pieces to each half sphere. Reserve about ½ cup of batter for later. I personally used an 8 half-sphere/compartment silicone mold.

6. Freeze the takoyaki batter for at least 1 hour or until it has completely firmed up.

7. Unmold the half sphere takoyaki by pressing the base of each sphere compartment. The takoyaki should pop right out of the silicone mold. Using the reserved batter, glue 2 half spheres to make 1 ball. Continue for the rest of your half spheres, then put the balls back in the mold and freezer for 10 minutes. This should give you a total of 5 takoyaki balls.

8. Place the oil in a large nonstick frying pan over medium heat. Add the takoyaki to the pan.

9. Fry for 5 minutes, until they are golden brown but are not 100 percent cooked through. The takoyaki should be slightly soft and gooey in the middle.

10. To make the takoyaki sauce, combine all the ingredients in a bowl and mix until the sugar has dissolved.

11. Serve your takoyaki piping hot, drizzled with your homemade takoyaki sauce, Kewpie Mayonnaise, bonito flakes, shredded nori, and the reserved green parts of the green onion.

TIP: *If buying fresh octopus, wash the octopus and remove the internal organs, including the ink sac and beak. All frozen octopus is precleaned.*

TIP: *If you are unable to find half-sphere silicone molds, ice cube trays will also work. However, you will not get that iconic takoyaki shape.*

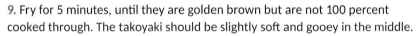

YAKISOBA PAN

FOR THE YAKISOBA:
5 dried shiitake mushrooms

1 (14-ounce) package ramen or yakisoba noodles

2 tablespoons oil

6 slices bacon or thinly sliced pork belly, cut into bite-size pieces

1 onion, finely sliced

1 cup julienned carrots

3 cups shredded green cabbage

1 tablespoon roughly chopped pickled red ginger

2 cloves garlic, minced

3 green onions, cut into 2-inch batons

1 cup deseeded and julienned yellow bell pepper

salt and pepper, to taste

FOR THE YAKISOBA SAUCE:
2 teaspoons brown sugar

2 teaspoons soy sauce

3 tablespoons oyster sauce

4 teaspoons ketchup or tomato sauce

4 tablespoons Worcestershire sauce

3 soft hot dog buns, sliced and buttered

thinly sliced pickled ginger, sliced green onions, drizzle of toasted sesame oil, sesame seeds, dried nori, and Kewpie Mayonnaise, for serving

Calling all carb lovers! *Yakisoba-pan*, or "fried noodles bread," is the ultimate Japanese street food. It combines two delicious carbs: savory Japanese stir-fried noodles stuffed between fluffy hot dog buns. I highly recommend this dish, but be careful not to turn into a pig in the process! This dish typically uses soba noodles and is flavored with condiments similar to Worcestershire sauce.

Yield: 3 servings | Prep time: 25 minutes | Cook time: 25 minutes

1. Place the dried shiitake mushrooms in a small bowl with boiling water and let them steep for 20 minutes. Once they are soft, drain and reserve 2 tablespoons of the mushroom water. Thinly slice the mushrooms and set aside.

2. In a medium bowl, whisk all the ingredients for the yakisoba sauce until the sugar has dissolved. Taste and add more sugar if required, as some ketchup has a lower sugar content. Set aside.

3. Cook the noodles according to the package instructions. Drain and set aside.

4. While the noodles are boiling, heat the oil over medium-high heat in a large pan or wok. Place the bacon into the pan and cook until it becomes crispy, about 7 minutes. Remove the bacon from the pan and set the bacon aside.

5. Using the bacon fat in the same pan, add the onion and carrots, and cook for 1 to 2 minutes. Add the cabbage and pickled ginger, and cook for an additional 3 minutes, until the vegetables are tender.

6. Add the minced garlic, green onion, yellow peppers, and shiitake mushrooms and cook for 2 minutes. Add the cooked ramen or yakisoba noodles to the pan and lower the heat to medium. Toss the noodles with the other ingredients in the pan using a pair of tongs and stir-fry for another 2 to 5 minutes. The noodles have a tendency to stick to the bottom of the pan, so move the noodles constantly, adding 1 or 2 tablespoons of oil as needed to prevent the noodles from sticking.

7. Finally, add the yakisoba sauce and toss to coat all the noodles. Season with salt and pepper, to taste.

8. Stuff the yakisoba noodles into your sliced and buttered hot dog buns.

9. Serve with thinly sliced pickled ginger, sliced green onions, a drizzle of toasted sesame oil, sesame seeds, dried nori, and Kewpie Mayonnaise.

TIP: *Use a large pan or wok so that the ingredients have more contact with the hot surface. This will create a nice char, which is a flavor booster. If you prefer ultra-crispy noodles, fry them immediately after cooking the bacon. Transfer them into another dish and start cooking the other ingredients.*

TIP: *If you are buying fresh yakisoba noodles, place the noodles in a bowl of warm water and gently try loosening the strands with your hands. This will prevent the noodles from breaking when stir-frying them.*

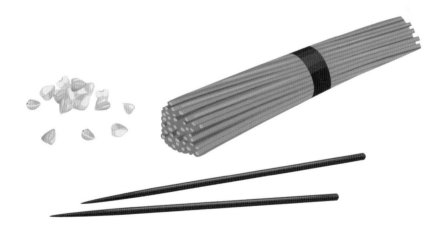

CRISPY PORK GYOZA

FOR THE GYOZA FILLING:
4 dried shiitake mushrooms

2 to 3 large green cabbage leaves, roughly chopped into small pieces

¾ pound ground pork

2 medium green onions, sliced

1 teaspoon grated ginger

1½ teaspoons soy sauce

1 teaspoon toasted sesame oil

1½ teaspoons dashi powder

2 cloves garlic, minced

3 teaspoons cornstarch or corn flour

¾ teaspoon salt

crack of black pepper

1 teaspoon sake

1 large egg

30 gyoza wrappers

2 tablespoons neutral-flavored oil

FOR THE GYOZA WINGS:
2 tablespoons corn flour or cornstarch

1 tablespoon all-purpose flour

¾ cup water

FOR THE DIPPING SAUCE:
¼ cup soy sauce

¼ cup rice wine vinegar

1 teaspoon sesame oil

1½ teaspoons honey

2 teaspoons mirin

These super-crispy, flavorful appetizers are a must-try when you visit the Spirit Realm—just remember to hurry back before dark!

Yield: 24 pieces | Prep time: 50 minutes | Cook time: 30 minutes

1. Place the dried shiitake mushrooms in a bowl of boiling water and let them soak for 20 minutes. Once they are soft, drain, dice, and set aside.

2. Place the cabbage leaves in a medium bowl and pour boiling water on them. Soak them for 5 minutes, until slightly softened, then shock in ice water to preserve the color. Drain and set aside.

3. In a medium bowl, combine the shiitake mushrooms, cabbage, ground pork, green onion, grated ginger, soy sauce, sesame oil, dashi powder, minced garlic, cornstarch, salt, freshly ground black pepper, and sake. Knead the mixture with your hands or a food processor until it becomes sticky and pale in color.

4. Crack the egg into a small bowl and whisk until well combined.

5. To fold the gyoza, take a wrapper and place 1½ teaspoons of the filling in the center. Moisten the edges of the gyoza wrapper with a bit of whisked egg. Fold the wrapper in half over the filling without sealing it. Pinch the center of the gyoza wrapper with your fingers. Using your thumb and index finger, pleat from the center to the right side. Press the pleats tightly so the filling won't spill out during the cooking process. Continue the same process starting from the center to the left side, then place the gyoza on a large plate that is lightly covered in flour. Repeat for the remaining gyoza wrappers.

6. Heat the oil in a large nonstick frying pan over high heat. Arrange 6 dumplings in the pan in a circular pattern. Cook for 3 minutes, or until they start to turn golden brown at the bottom. Flip and cook the other side for another minute.

7. Combine the ingredients for the gyoza wings in a small bowl.

8. Pour ¼ of the gyoza wing mixture over the gyoza. Cover, reduce the heat to low, and cook for 5 minutes, until the water has evaporated.

9. Gently loosen the gyoza with a spatula and cook for another minute, uncovered. Repeat the frying process for the remaining gyoza (4 batches total).

10. Alternatively, you can omit the gyoza wing mixture and add 3 tablespoons of water to the pan once the gyoza bases have browned. Cover and cook for 5 minutes. Serve the gyoza separately on a serving plate.

11. Finally, combine the dipping sauce ingredients in a small bowl.

12. Serve the dumplings hot with the dipping sauce.

TIP: *These are great if you are busy at work and need a quick snack.*

TIP: *Once all the gyoza have been pleated and sealed, they can be frozen for a month. Place the gyoza on a lined baking sheet (making sure that they are not touching each other) and flash freeze them by placing them in the freezer for 1 to 2 hours or until frozen solid. Transfer them to a bag.*

CHICKEN KARAAGE

2 tablespoons soy sauce

2 tablespoons sake

juice of 1 tablespoon grated ginger

1 clove garlic, finely grated

1 tablespoon brown sugar

1 tablespoon mirin

1 teaspoon pepper

1⅓ pounds boneless skin-on chicken thighs, cut into bite-size pieces

4 cups neutral-flavored oil, for shallow frying

1 cup potato starch or cornstarch

sea salt, to taste

togarashi, Kewpie Mayonnaise, and lemon wedges, for serving

shredded cabbage, optional

This fried chicken is a favorite among certain faceless spirits. Unlike American fried chicken, *karaage* uses boneless fillets that have been coated in potato or cornstarch rather than in a batter. Another signature difference is that *karaage* imparts more soy sauce and mirin flavors in the actual chicken due to the marinating process.

Yield: 3 to 4 servings (6 pieces per serving) | Prep time: 15 minutes, plus 30 minutes to overnight to marinate | Cook time: 35 to 40 minutes

1. Combine the soy sauce, sake, juice of the grated ginger, garlic, brown sugar, mirin, and pepper in a small bowl. Stir until the sugar has dissolved.

2. Pour the marinade over the chicken. Let the chicken marinate in the fridge for at least 30 minutes up to overnight.

3. Add the oil to a wok or deep frying pan over medium-high heat. Heat the oil until it reaches 350°F.

4. Toss the marinated chicken in the potato starch or cornstarch. Shake off the excess starch.

5. Add a small batch of the chicken to the hot oil and fry for 3 minutes, until the pieces are nearly cooked through. Set them aside and let rest while you fry the other chicken pieces.

6. Return the fried chicken to the oil and fry for another 3 to 4 minutes, until it is crispy and golden brown. Place it on a wire rack so that air can circulate at the bottom of the chicken. While it is still hot, sprinkle on sea salt, to taste.

7. Serve the chicken karaage in a newspaper cone and top it with a combination of togorashi, Kewpie Mayonnaise, and lemon wedges.

OKONOMIYAKI

2 cups all-purpose flour

4 tablespoons corn flour or cornstarch

½ teaspoon salt

½ teaspoon sugar

½ teaspoon baking powder

1½ cups dashi stock, room temperature

2 large eggs

½ cup fried tenkasu, or tempura scraps (optional, see the Classic Tempura Selection tip on page 53)

1 medium green onion, sliced

2 tablespoons pickled red ginger, chopped, plus extra for garnishing

½ medium head green cabbage, finely shredded

2 tablespoons neutral-flavored oil

6 strips bacon

6 medium raw tiger shrimp, shelled and deveined (optional)

FOR THE OKONOMIYAKI SAUCE:
2 tablespoons ketchup

1 tablespoon soy sauce

2 tablespoons Worcestershire sauce

1 tablespoon honey

Kewpie Mayonnaise, sesame seeds, togarashi spice, shredded nori, and bonito flakes, for garnishing

This savory pancake is a popular dish from the streets of Osaka, Japan. Made from flour, eggs, shredded cabbage, and your choice of protein, it is topped with an assortment of condiments. The literal translation of *okonomiyaki* is "grilled as you like." A highly recommended bar snack among the residents of a particular valley. Just ask the frog residents next to you.

Yield: 6 servings, 1 pancake per serving | Prep time: 25 minutes | Cook time: 30 minutes

1. In a large bowl, combine the flour, corn flour or cornstarch, salt, sugar, and baking powder. Mix until well combined.

2. Add the dashi stock to the flour mixture. Whisk until combined, then let it rest for 15 minutes in the fridge while the gluten develops.

3. To make the okonomiyaki sauce, combine all the ingredients in a medium bowl and mix until the sugar dissolves. Set aside.

4. Take the batter out of the refrigerator and add the eggs, tempura scraps, if using, green onion, and pickled ginger. Mix well.

5. Add half the shredded cabbage to the batter and mix well, until the batter coats most of the cabbage pieces. Add the remaining cabbage to the mixture.

6. Heat the oil in a medium nonstick pan over medium heat. When the oil is hot, pour the batter into the pan, forming a 3-inch circle. Place 2 slices of bacon on top of the okonomiyaki and cook, covered, for 5 minutes. Another alternative is to swap the bacon with 2 pieces of shrimp per pancake.

7. When the bottom becomes crispy and golden, flip the okonomiyaki and gently flatten it with a spatula to a ½-inch thickness. Cook, covered, for another 5 minutes. Flip and cook, uncovered, for 2 minutes more.

8. Repeat with the remaining mixture, wiping the skillet and brushing on more oil as needed. In total, you should have 6 large pancakes.

9. Drizzle the okonomiyaki with the sauce and thin strips of Kewpie Mayonnaise squeezed from its container. Top with sesame seeds, pickled red ginger, bonito flakes, togarashi spice, and nori. Serve hot.

TIP: *Okonomiyaki is so versatile, it's easy to get creative with this recipe. Include calamari, dried shrimp, cheese, octopus, corn, kimchi, or yakisoba noodles—the list is endless.*

TONKATSU

¼ head green cabbage, finely shredded

4 pieces pork tenderloin (2 pounds in total), deboned

1½ teaspoons salt

¼ teaspoon freshly ground black pepper

½ teaspoon Chinese five-spice powder

½ cup all-purpose flour

2 large eggs, beaten

1 cup panko breadcrumbs

4 cups neutral-flavored oil, for frying

FOR THE TONKATSU SAUCE:
1½ tablespoons Worcestershire sauce

⅓ cup ketchup

2 tablespoons soy sauce

1 tablespoon oyster sauce

1 tablespoon brown sugar

lemon slices, for serving

Juicy on the inside and crunchy on the outside, *tonkatsu* (a pork chop breaded with panko and fried) is one of those simple comfort foods that can be enjoyed for lunch or dinner. A perfect meal to be enjoyed before heading back to the bathhouse and tending to your guests.

Yield: 4 servings | Prep time: 20 minutes | Cook time: 20 minutes

1. Soak the shredded cabbage in cold water for 5 minutes and drain. This will retain the color and crunch.

2. To prepare the pork, make several slits on the edge of the pork (white area between the meat and fat). This will prevent the pork tenderloin from curling when deep frying. Place the pork between 2 sheets of plastic wrap and pound using a mallet until each piece is ½-inch thick.

3. Season both sides of the pork with salt, pepper, and five-spice powder. Set aside.

4. For the dredging process, keep separate medium bowls for the flour, eggs, and panko breadcrumbs.

5. Dip the pork in the following order: flour, eggs, and panko breadcrumbs. Press the breadcrumbs into the pork to evenly coat each piece.

6. Heat about 1 inch of oil in a large nonstick frying pan or wok over medium-high heat. Fry the pork for 4 to 5 minutes on each side, or until golden and cooked throughout. The pork should not be pink in the middle.

7. Drain the pork on a wire rack. Repeat for the rest of the pork cutlets.

8. Combine the sauce ingredients in a medium bowl and stir until the sugar has dissolved.

9. Slice the tonkatsu into 1-inch strips and serve warm with the prepared sauce, shredded cabbage, and a slice of lemon.

KATSUDON

⅔ cup dashi stock

1 tablespoon sake

2 teaspoons sugar

1 tablespoon soy sauce

1 tablespoon mirin

2 large eggs

2 tablespoons neutral-flavored oil

1 medium onion, sliced, divided

2 pieces leftover tonkatsu (see page 75 if you are making it from scratch), sliced

salt and pepper, to taste

2 medium bowls freshly cooked jasmine rice

1 medium green onion, sliced, for garnishing

togarashi, for serving (optional)

Katsudon is a dish that consists of tonkatsu served over steamy rice with onion and egg. If you ever have leftover tonkatsu in the fridge, this recipe is a perfect way to turn it into a wholesome meal on a busy weekday.

Yield: 2 servings | Prep time: 5 minutes | Cook time: 15 minutes

1. In a medium bowl, combine the dashi stock, sake, sugar, soy sauce, and mirin. In a separate small bowl, lightly beat the 2 eggs and set aside.

2. Heat the oil in a large nonstick frying pan over medium heat. Add half the sliced onion and fry until it is translucent and slightly caramelized. This should take about 7 minutes.

3. Pour half the dashi mixture over the onion and let simmer for 1 to 2 minutes.

4. Add half the sliced tonkatsu over the onion and drizzle half of the egg mixture on top and into the sides of the pan. Cook over medium-low heat until the eggs have just set, about 2 to 3 minutes, and set aside. Repeat the process for the other tonkatsu. Add salt and pepper, to taste.

5. Serve the hot tonkatsu egg mixture in two plates over steamy jasmine rice and garnish with sliced green onions. Add the togarashi seasoning for some extra heat if desired.

CHAPTER 5
DESSERTS AND BAKERY TREATS

HOT HONEYED MILK

1½ cups whole milk

1 cinnamon stick, broken in half

1 heaping tablespoon honey

pinch of ground cinnamon

This sweet treat will be sure to warm you and mysterious new fishy friends on a dark and stormy night while your dad is looking for you. I would also cross the sea for this sweet beverage. Serve hot and blow on it a couple of times before you enjoy your first sip (or big gulp).

Yield: 1 serving | Prep time: 5 minutes | Cook time: 5 minutes

1. To a small pot over medium to low heat, add the milk and bring it to a boil. Be careful not to burn the milk or let it bubble over.

2. Once the milk has been brought up to a boil, turn off the stove and add the cinnamon stick. Let it steep in the hot milk for 4 minutes, then remove.

3. Pour the hot milk into a mug and add the honey. Stir until the honey has dissolved.

4. Sprinkle with a pinch of ground cinnamon and enjoy warm.

TIP: *If you are vegan or lactose intolerant, coconut milk is a great alternative and adds more tropical flavors to this beverage.*

TIP: *Add less or more honey according to your taste.*

REWARDING AND DECADENT CHOCOLATE CAKE

FOR THE CAKE BATTER:

2 cups cake flour

1¼ cups superfine sugar

7 tablespoons unsalted butter

½ cup neutral-flavored oil

3 tablespoons dark cocoa powder

½ teaspoon espresso powder

1 cup water

2 eggs, lightly beaten

1 teaspoon baking soda

1 teaspoon vanilla extract

½ cup buttermilk*

pinch of salt

FOR THE CHOCOLATE SYRUP:

¼ cup superfine sugar

2 tablespoons water

1 tablespoon dark cocoa powder

3 tablespoons fresh cream

FOR THE CHOCOLATE BUTTERCREAM:

1½ sticks plus ½ tablespoon unsalted butter, softened

2½ cups powdered sugar

¼ cup dark cocoa powder

1 tablespoon vanilla extract

3 tablespoons whole milk

FOR THE CHOCOLATE GANACHE:

¼ cup heavy cream
7 ounces dark chocolate, chopped into small pieces

FOR THE CAKE DECORATIONS:

6 ounces white chocolate

red and green chocolate food color, typically in powder form

This is the ultimate gooey chocolate cake. It's the perfect treat for chocolate lovers of all ages and even makes a great reward for a broomstick delivery job well done.

Yield: 6 to 8 servings | Prep time: 45 minutes | Cook time: 20 to 25 minutes

FOR THE CAKE BATTER

1. Preheat the oven to 350°F.

2. Mix together the flour and sugar in a medium bowl.

3. In a separate small pot over medium heat, add the butter, oil, dark cocoa powder, espresso powder, and water. Remove from the heat once it has been brought up to a boil, then let cool for 2 minutes.

4. Combine the cocoa mixture with your dry ingredients and mix until well incorporated.

5. Combine the eggs, baking soda, vanilla extract, and buttermilk in a separate medium bowl. Add the wet ingredients to the dry ingredients and whisk until well incorporated. Try not to overmix it as the cake will become dense and fragile to stack.

6. Line the bottom of two 9-inch round cake pans with parchment paper and apply cooking spray on the sides to make sure that the cake does not stick. Evenly distribute the batter between the 2 pans. Wrap damp strips of cloth around the perimeter of the cake tins, securing it with a metal safety pin. This will prevent your cake from doming too much.

7. Place the 2 cake pans on the same rack in the middle of the oven and bake your cakes for 20 to 25 minutes. (If you are unable to bake the 2 cakes on the same rack, place 1 cake pan on the bottom and 1 cake pan on the top rack diagonally from each other to create airflow—the cakes should not be directly over one another. At the 18-minute mark, swap the pans for even cooking.) When a toothpick inserted in the center of the cake comes out clean, it is done.

8. Unwrap the cloths around the cake tins and loosen the edges of the cake from the pan using a butter knife. Place a large plate over the pan and invert to release the cake from the pan. Remove the parchment paper from the bottom of the cake and let the cake cool. Repeat for the other cake pan.

FOR THE CHOCOLATE SYRUP

1. While your cake is baking, add the sugar and water to a pot over medium to low heat. Boil for 5 minutes, until it has slightly thickened.

2. Remove the pot from the heat and stir in the cocoa powder and cream. Mix until dissolved. Let it cool for 2 to 3 minutes. The sauce will further thicken as it cools down.

3. While the cake is still warm, poke holes into it with a toothpick. Spoon the chocolate syrup over the surface of the cake. The cake will absorb this chocolate syrup, giving it that moist and gooey texture. Repeat for the other cake.

FOR THE CHOCOLATE BUTTERCREAM

1. Using an electric mixer on medium to high speed, mix together the softened butter, icing sugar, cocoa powder, vanilla extract, and milk until well combined. Taste the icing to ensure it is sweet enough. The buttercream icing should be light and fluffy.

FOR THE CHOCOLATE GANACHE

1. In a small pot over medium heat, bring your cream to a boil.

2. Place the dark chocolate pieces in a bowl. Pour the cream over them and mix until the chocolate has melted and is well incorporated. Set aside.

FOR THE CAKE DECORATIONS

1. Place a ceramic bowl over a pot of simmering water (make sure the bottom of the bowl does not touch the water). Add the chopped white chocolate and let it melt completely. Divide your melted chocolate between 3 bowls and add your red and green food coloring separately to the chocolate in 2 bowls. Place the melted chocolate into 3 separate piping bags.

2. Using the white chocolate, pipe the lettering "Kiki" and the outline of the witch onto a sheet of parchment paper. For the tree, pipe using green food coloring. Finally, pipe Kiki's bow using the red melted chocolate. Place the chocolate pieces into the fridge to firm up for 15 minutes.

TO ASSEMBLE

1. Once your cakes have cooled completely, level them by cutting the top part of the cake where it forms a dome.

2. Spread the buttercream icing in between your cakes and stack them on a cake board or large dish.

3. Using a palette knife, lightly cover the entire cake in the buttercream icing and set it aside in the fridge for 30 to 45 minutes until it has cooled.

4. Once the cake has cooled completely, place the cake on a wired rack and pour the chocolate ganache over it. Let the cake set in the fridge for 15 more minutes.

5. Place your chocolate pieces on the cake and serve with a warm cup of tea or coffee.

TIP: *If you do not have buttermilk available, combine ½ cup of fresh milk with 2 teaspoons of lemon juice. Let the mixture sit for 10 minutes, and the milk will start to curdle slightly.*

TEA PARTY SPRITZ COOKIES

1¾ sticks softened butter

½ cup superfine sugar

1 large egg

1 teaspoon vanilla extract

2½ cups cake flour

½ teaspoon salt

¼ cup cocoa powder

8 glacé cherries, halved

These buttery, sweet cookies get their intricate design from a cookie press and can be decorated with just about anything. They make the perfect reward for young girls who return stolen items to you. Best served with the Tea Party Mini Gelatin (page 86) and the Tea Party Cantonese Egg Cake (page 87) while you wait for a certain water dragon to arrive.

Yield: 50 cookies | Prep time: 25 minutes | Cook time: 15 minutes

1. Preheat the oven to 350°F. Line two 9 x 13-inch baking sheets with parchment paper or silicone mats.

2. In a large mixing bowl of a stand mixer with a paddle attachment, cream the butter and sugar on medium-high speed until the mixture becomes pale and creamy.

3. Add the egg and vanilla extract, and beat on high speed until combined. Scrape down the sides with a silicone spatula and beat once more until combined.

4. With the mixer on low speed, slowly add in the flour and salt. Switch to medium speed and beat until well combined.

5. Divide the dough in half and place one portion of the dough in a separate bowl. Set aside.

6. Add the cocoa powder to the remaining dough left in the stand mixer bowl. Mix until well combined.

7. Press the cocoa-flavored dough into the cookie press with the star plate (follow the manufacturer's guide to fit and use the cookie press with the decorative plate). Hold the cookie press perpendicular to the lined baking sheets and press out the cookies. Make sure to keep them 2 inches apart, as they will spread. Decorate by lightly pressing a halved glacé cherry at the center of each flower cookie.

8. Roll out the remaining dough to ½-inch thick on a work surface dusted with flour. Using a decorative square cookie cutter with wavy edges, cut out the shapes and place them on the baking tray. Score hatches across the cookie.

9. Bake both cookies for 10 to 15 minutes until they are lightly golden brown.

10. Remove the cookies from the oven and allow them to cool on the baking sheet for 5 minutes before transferring them to a wire rack to cool completely.

TIP: *If your cookie dough becomes too soft to handle, place it back in the refrigerator and chill for 15 minutes.*

TIP: *Spritz cookies are similar to sugar cookies; however, the key characteristic is to use a cookie press to get their decorative and detailed shapes. If you do not have a cookie press, you can also use a piping bag fitted with an open star tip. Add a bit of milk to the cookie dough to make it easier to pipe.*

TIP: *If desired, you can also drizzle melted chocolate or use sprinkles to decorate the cookies.*

TIP: *There is no need to grease the baking sheets, as the butter from the cookies will make it easier to release them from the pan.*

TEA PARTY MINI GELATIN

2 packets gelatin (1 cherry and 1 greengage flavored)

2 cups hot water

2 cups cold water

These delightfully fun and jiggly mini gelatin snacks are the perfect addition to any tea party! Be sure to serve with the Tea Party Spritz Cookies (page 85) and the Tea Party Cantonese Egg Cake (page 87).

Yield: 5 to 6 servings | Prep time: 2½ hours to set | Cook time: 5 minutes

1. Place 1 packet of flavored gelatin into a medium mixing bowl with a spout. Pour in 1 cup of hot water and stir until the sugar has dissolved.

2. Pour in 1 cup of cold water and mix until combined. Pour the jelly into greased mini tart pans (similar to those used to make the Portuguese egg tarts).

3. Repeat the same process for the other packet of jelly.

4. Place the jelly molds into the refrigerator and chill for 2½ hours or until they have firmed up.

5. To release the jelly from the molds, place the bottom of the molds in a bowl of boiling water and hold for 5 to 10 seconds.

6. Serve chilled, with the Cantonese egg cake and spritz cookies.

TIP: *If you are unable to find cherry or greengage-flavored jellos, you can use strawberry and lime jello packets instead.*

TEA PARTY CANTONESE EGG CAKE

8 large eggs

1½ cups superfine sugar

½ cup water

2 tablespoons oil

2 cups cake flour

1¼ teaspoons baking powder

My mother is famously known for her Cantonese steamed cake among the Chinese community in South Africa. A childhood favorite of mine, this superlight and fluffy cake with no frills or icing is definitely worth sharing with your newfound faceless friend at a witch's cottage!

Yield: 6 to 8 servings, 1 slice per serving | Prep time: 20 minutes | Cook time: 30 minutes

1. In an electric mixer, beat the eggs on high speed for 5 minutes, until light and pale.

2. Add the sugar and beat for another 5 minutes on high speed.

3. Gradually add in the water and oil.

4. Lower the speed to medium low and slowly add the flour and baking powder. Beat until smooth and the flour is well incorporated.

5. Line a 9-inch bamboo steamer with parchment paper and pour in the cake mixture. Any size bamboo steamer will do, but it needs to be small enough to fit into a pot.

6. Place a wire rack at the bottom of an 11-inch or wider pot, then add boiling water (the water should not touch the bottom of the bamboo steamer). Lower your bamboo steamer onto the wire rack and wrap the pot lid in a kitchen tea towel to capture the water droplets when steaming.

7. Steam on high heat for 30 minutes, or until a toothpick inserted into the cake comes out clean.

CHEESE AND ONION FISH CRACKERS

1 cup shredded Gouda, cheddar, or any sharp, hard cheese of your choice

1 cup all-purpose flour

2 tablespoons parmesan cheese

½ teaspoon baking powder

3 medium green onions (green parts only), finely diced

¼ cup whole milk

1 tablespoon neutral-flavored vegetable oil

2 tablespoons sesame seeds (optional)

crack of black pepper, for seasoning

Cheese and Onion Fish Crackers are a delicious mini snack that may help you if you ever want to win over the cat prince's heart. These crackers are not suitable for animals. You can find the pet-friendly Tuna Fish Crackers on page 90.

Yield: 60 crackers | Prep time: 20 minutes | Cook time: 15 minutes

1. In a medium bowl, combine the hard cheese, flour, parmesan, baking powder, and green onions until the cheese is evenly distributed.

2. Add the milk and vegetable oil, and mix with a spatula. Knead the mixture with your hands until a dough ball forms. If the dough is dry, add 1 tablespoon of water. If the dough is too wet, add 2 tablespoons of flour. Let the dough rest at room temperature for 10 to 15 minutes.

3. Preheat the oven to 375°F. Line 2 baking sheets with parchment paper or silicone mats.

4. Turn the dough out onto a floured surface and divide it in half. Working with 1 section, roll the dough as thin as possible, preferably to ¼-inch thick. The thinner the crackers are, the crispier they will be. You can also roll out the dough a bit thicker if you want it to have some chew and a breadlike consistency.

5. Using a cookie cutter, stamp out the dough into fish shapes. Repeat for the remainder of the dough. Reroll the scraps of dough and stamp more fish shapes.

6. Carefully transfer the crackers to the prepared baking sheets, spacing them an inch apart. Sprinkle with sesame seeds, if desired. Using a toothpick or the blunt end of a skewer, make holes for the eyes and markings for the gills.

7. Bake for 10 minutes, or until the crackers are crispy and golden along the edges. The timing may vary, depending on the size of your crackers. At the 10-minute mark, flip the fish crackers with a spatula and bake for 5 more minutes, until golden.

8. Transfer the crackers to a wire rack and let them cool completely. Store in an airtight container for up to 1 week.

TIP: *Be creative with the seasonings. You can add smoked paprika, onion powder, parsley, or chile flakes to the dough mixture.*

TUNA FISH CRACKERS
(FOR YOUR FELINE FRIENDS)

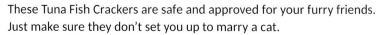

1 (4-ounce) can tuna, drained

1 large egg

1½ cups whole wheat flour

1 tablespoon sesame seeds (optional)

These Tuna Fish Crackers are safe and approved for your furry friends. Just make sure they don't set you up to marry a cat.

Yield: 3 to 4 servings | Prep time: 20 minutes | Cook time: 20 minutes

1. In a medium bowl, combine the tuna, egg, and flour until combined. Knead the mixture with your hands until a dough ball forms. If the dough is dry, add 1 tablespoon of water. If the dough is too wet, add 2 tablespoons of flour. Let the dough rest at room temperature for 10 to 15 minutes.

2. Turn the dough out onto a floured surface and divide it in half. Working with 1 section, roll the dough as thin as possible, preferably to ¼-inch thick. Stamp out the dough into fish shapes using a cookie cutter. Repeat for the remainder of the dough.

3. Preheat the oven to 375°F. Line 2 baking sheets with parchment paper or silicone mats.

4. Carefully transfer the crackers onto the prepared baking sheets, spacing them 1 inch apart. Sprinkle with sesame seeds, if desired. Using a toothpick or the blunt end of a skewer, make holes for the eyes and markings for the gills.

5. Bake for 10 minutes, or until the crackers are crispy and golden on the edges. The timing may vary, depending on the size of your crackers. At the 10-minute mark, flip the fish cookies using a spatula and bake for 8 more minutes, ensuring they are golden on the other side. These should be crunchy when they are done.

6. Transfer the crackers onto a wire rack and let them cool completely. Store in a container for up to 1 week.

TIP: *Add ½ teaspoon of catnip or thyme to the dough for some extra flavor. While humans can eat these crackers, they will taste bland as they do not contain salt or other seasonings.*

TIP: *Disclaimer: Cats can be picky—you can't win all of them over with these treats.*

DUO THUMBPRINT COOKIES

FOR THE COOKIE DOUGH:

⅔ cup softened salted butter

½ cup granulated brown sugar

1 large egg

1 teaspoon vanilla extract

1¾ cups cake flour

½ teaspoon salt

1 teaspoon baking powder

FOR THE STRAWBERRY VARIATION:

½ cup granulated white sugar

½ cup strawberry jam

FOR THE APRICOT VARIATION:

½ cup unsweetened, finely shredded coconut

½ cup apricot jam

These thumbprint cookies have a soft, chewy texture, are coated with a crunchy sugar or coconut exterior, and have jam-filled centers. Pack these with some grape juice and have a late-night picnic while rowing across the lagoon.

Yield: 30 cookies | Prep time: 20 minutes, plus 30 to 45 minutes to chill | Cook time: 15 minutes

1. Using a stand mixer or a handheld mixer on medium to high speed, cream the butter and sugar in a large bowl until the mixture becomes pale and fluffy, 3 to 5 minutes.

2. Add the egg and vanilla extract to the butter mixture and beat until combined.

3. In a separate medium bowl, combine the flour, salt, and baking powder.

4. Add your dry ingredients to your wet ingredients and beat on medium to high speed until the dough is well mixed and smooth. If the dough is too sticky, add 1 tablespoon of flour at a time. If the dough is too dry, add 1 tablespoon of water at a time. Continue to add more or less flour or water until you have reached the desired consistency. The dough should be malleable and easy to roll into mini balls.

5. Divide the dough into 30 equal pieces and roll each piece into 1-inch balls.

6. For the strawberry variation, roll the balls in a small bowl of granulated sugar and set them aside

7. For the apricot variation, roll the balls in a small bowl of finely shredded unsweetened coconut and set them aside.

8. Using your thumb or a measuring teaspoon, make a small indention in the center of the raw cookie dough. Repeat for the remaining dough balls.

9. Place the 2 variations of cookie dough on 2 baking trays lined with a silicone mat or parchment paper. Ensure each cookie is spaced 1½ inches apart. Place the 2 baking trays in the refrigerator and let the dough chill for 30 to 45 minutes. This will ensure that the cookies hold their shape and won't spread out too much during the baking process. After the cookie dough has chilled, preheat the oven to 375°F.

10. Spoon 1 teaspoon of strawberry jam into the indentation in each cookie coated in granulated sugar. Spoon 1 teaspoon of apricot jam into the indentation of each cookie coated in coconut.

11. Bake for 15 minutes, until the edges of the cookies turn golden brown. To ensure even baking (cookies are golden on all edges), rotate the baking tray at the 10-minute mark and continue baking. Remove from the oven and cool on the baking tray for 10 minutes, then carefully transfer the cookies to a wire rack to cool completely.

SIBERIA CAKE

Red bean paste sandwiched between two soft, jiggly, eggy sponge layers. Wrapped in newspaper, these are perfect with some English tea to get you inspired to design fighter planes. It's guaranteed that this will taste better than that of the train station's street vendor.

Yield: 4 servings, 1 slice per serving | Prep time: 30 minutes | Cook time: 1 hour, 20 minutes

FOR THE CASTELLA SPONGE CAKE:

½ cup butter

¾ cup whole milk

7 large eggs

¾ cup plus 1 tablespoon bread flour

1 teaspoon vanilla extract

1 teaspoon lemon zest

1 teaspoon lemon juice

¾ cup superfine sugar

FOR THE RED BEAN FILLING:

½ cup water

1 tablespoon gelatin powder

1 pound red bean paste (see the Red Bean Bao recipe on page 95 if you want to make this from scratch)

1. In a small pot over low heat, whisk the butter and milk until combined and the butter has melted fully. Set aside.

2. Separate the egg whites and egg yolks into 2 bowls—whites in 1 bowl, yolks in another.

3. Into a large bowl, sift the flour. Add the warm butter-milk mixture and stir until well combined. Slowly add in 1 egg yolk at a time and mix, until the batter becomes thicker. Stir in the vanilla extract and lemon zest.

4. In a medium bowl of a stand mixer, add the lemon juice to the egg whites and whip until foamy. The lemon juice will stabilize the egg whites so that they will not collapse. Slowly start adding the sugar to the egg whites and whip the mixture until medium peaks form. Your whipped egg whites should hold their shape very well, but the tip of the peaks should curl over when you lift the beaters.

5. In 3 separate portions, fold the egg-white mixture into the batter using a spatula, until just combined. Do not overmix.

6. Pour the batter into 2 greased and lined 4 x 8.5-inch rectangular cake pans. Lightly drag a toothpick through the batter in a zigzag motion to get rid of any of the air bubbles. Place the pan into a larger baking tray and add warm to hot water (not boiling) to the tray so that ⅓ of the cake pans are submerged.

7. Bake in a preheated oven at 300°F for 1 hour, or until a toothpick comes out clean when inserted in the center of the cake. Let cool in the baking pan for 10 minutes. Loosen the edges of the cake with a butter knife and turn them out onto a wire rack. Remove the parchment paper from the cakes and let them cool completely.

8. To make the red bean filling, while the cake is baking, add the water to a medium pot and bring it to a boil over high heat. Add the gelatin powder and mix until it has dissolved. Add the red bean paste to the mixture and stir until it becomes thick and glossy. Allow to cool slightly.

9. To assemble the Siberia Cake, spread a ½-inch-thick layer of red bean filling evenly over 1 of the cake layers. Let it chill in the fridge for 15 to 30 minutes, then place the second cake layer over the red bean filling, pressing gently so the layers stick together. Chill for another 15 to 30 minutes.

10. Trim the edges of the cake and cut the cake in half so you have 2 thick square cakes. Thereafter, cut the squares into triangles resembling sandwiches. Serve warm or cold wrapped in newspaper with a side of English tea.

TIP: *For a vegan substitute, add 2 tablespoons of agar powder instead of gelatin.*

TIP: *Make sure that the butter-milk-flour mixture is not too hot before adding the egg yolks.*

RED BEAN BAO

FOR THE RED BEAN FILLING:

1 cup dried red beans

2 cups water

¼ cup brown sugar

¼ cup honey

½ teaspoon salt

1½ teaspoons vanilla extract

6 cups water, for steaming

FOR THE BAO DOUGH:

1 cup warm water

3 tablespoons sugar

1½ teaspoons instant dry yeast

2½ cups cake flour

½ teaspoon salt

1 tablespoon neutral-flavored oil

1 teaspoon baking powder

These soft, pillowy buns filled with a sweet red bean filling are a popular Chinese dessert. They're the perfect treat for train-watching after a long day at the bathhouse.

Yield: 10 to 12 buns | Prep time: 13½ hours, including soaking and rising time | Cook time: 15 minutes

1. Wash and soak the dried red beans for 10 hours or overnight. They will double in size and yield around 2 cups of red beans.

2. To make the bao dough, combine the warm water and sugar in a small bowl until well combined. Add the yeast to the water-sugar mixture and stir. Leave the bowl in a warm, draft-free location until the mixture becomes frothy (similar to the froth in a cappuccino).

3. Sift the flour and salt into a large bowl. Make a well in the middle and add the oil and yeast mixture. Stir until it forms a rough dough.

4. Using the palm of your hands, knead the dough for 10 minutes, until the surface becomes smooth and elastic.

5. Place the dough in a well-oiled medium bowl, cover, and leave to rise in a warm place for 2 to 3 hours, until it has doubled in size.

6. While the dough is rising, drain the soaked red beans and place them in a pressure cooker. Add 2 cups of water and pressure cook on the bean setting (approximately 1 hour) until the beans are tender. If you do not have a pressure cooker, you can do this over the stove in a large pot over medium-high heat.

7. Add the sugar, honey, salt, and vanilla extract to the red bean mixture and roughly mash it with a potato masher. Place the pressure cooker on sauté mode and stir for a few minutes until the sugar has dissolved and the mixture becomes thick and glossy. Remove from the heat and set aside to cool.

8. Once the dough has risen, place it onto a floured surface and flatten it into a round disk. Add the baking powder to the center, fold up the dough, and knead for another 5 minutes.

9. Divide the dough into 10 to 12 even pieces, rolled out into 4-inch disks. Make sure to roll the edges of each disk slightly thinner.

10. Place a tablespoon of the red bean filling in the center of each circle. Gather the edges of the dough and bring them together, enclosing the filling. Twist to seal the dough.

11. Place the buns onto squares pieces of parchment paper, making sure the twisted side is facing downward. Your buns should be smooth on the top. Place the buns at least 1 inch apart in a bamboo steamer and allow them to rise an additional 20 to 30 minutes in a warm place.

12. While the dough is rising, at the 23-minute mark, place 6 cups water into a wok and bring it up to a rapid boil. Make sure there is enough water to steam the buns but not enough to touch the bottom of the bamboo steamer.

13. Place the bamboo steamer over the wok, ensuring the bamboo steamer fits tightly on the edges of the wok, and steam for approximately 10 to 15 minutes, or until the buns have risen and the dough has fully cooked. Treat the buns similarly to a cake, so no peeking during the steaming process as they will deflate due to the sudden drop in temperature.

14. Serve warm or at room temperature.

TIP: If the yeast mixture does not froth, this indicates that the yeast has not been activated or is too old. I suggest discarding the mixture and starting fresh.

TIP: I usually double or triple the red bean mixture and store it in the freezer (it can keep up to 6 months) if I ever want to use it for additional delicious red bean recipes. You can find more uses for it in the Red Bean Croissant (page 106) and Siberia Cake recipes (page 93).

TIP: If you are making this in winter and need a warm place to let your dough rise, I suggest turning your oven on at 375°F for 5 minutes. Immediately turn it off and place your dough inside the oven with the door closed. This will act as an insulating environment.

PUMPKIN BREAD

FOR THE PUMPKIN SPICE MIXTURE:

2 teaspoons ground cinnamon

½ teaspoon ground nutmeg

½ teaspoon ground ginger

½ teaspoon ground cloves or allspice

FOR THE SPICED PUMPKIN PUREE:

¼ cup brown sugar

2 tablespoons honey

2½ cups canned pumpkin puree or fresh steamed, cubed, and blended pumpkin or butternut squash

FOR THE BREAD:

1 tablespoon superfine sugar

⅓ cup warm water

2¼ teaspoons instant dry yeast

2½ cups bread flour

1 teaspoon salt

2 tablespoons melted butter, plus more for brushing

2 large eggs, divided

pumpkin seeds, for garnishing

This is the perfect baking recipe for the Halloween season (or any time you're feeling particularly witchy). Perhaps an aviation fanatic in a striped shirt will present one to you as a devotion of his love.

Yield: 8 to 10 buns | Prep time: 3½ hours | Cook time: 20 minutes

1. In a medium bowl, combine all the ingredients for your pumpkin spice mixture and set it aside.

2. In a separate large bowl, add the brown sugar, honey, and 2 teaspoons of your pumpkin spice mixture to the pumpkin or squash puree and stir until the sugar has dissolved. Add more honey or sugar, to taste. (You will have leftover pumpkin spice, which you can save to make this recipe again.)

3. To make the bread, mix the sugar and water until the sugar has dissolved. Sprinkle the instant dry yeast into the water mixture and mix until the yeast is blended in. Let sit for 5 to 10 minutes. The yeast will be activated and the mixture will become frothy.

4. Using the dough hook attachment of a stand mixer, combine the bread flour, yeast mixture, salt, ½ cup of pumpkin puree, butter, and 1 egg. On a low setting, mix to incorporate until the dough forms a ball. Once it has formed a ball, turn the stand mixer to medium speed and knead for 5 to 7 minutes. The dough will be slightly sticky but should be springy when you lightly press it with your thumb.

5. Place the dough in a greased bowl. Cover the bowl tightly with plastic wrap and leave it to rise in a warm place for 45 minutes to 1½ hours, until it has doubled in size.

6. Place the dough onto a floured working surface, divide it into 8 to 10 equal portions, and lightly knead each portion for 1 minute. Form each piece into a ball.

7. Using a rolling pin, roll out the first ball into a flat disk (it should not be too thin) and place 1 tablespoon of the pumpkin puree mixture in the center. Take the edges of the dough and stretch to encase the filling. Pinch and twist to seal the filling in the dough. Take the ball and tie it loosely with a 23-inch-long piece of kitchen string in such a way that the dough ball is divided into 8 sections while the dough ball remains intact. Make a tight knot at the end and place it on a flat baking tray. Repeat with the rest of the balls, ensuring they are spaced 1½ inches apart and let them rest in a warm place for 30 minutes to puff up slightly.

8. Preheat the oven to 350°F. In a separate bowl, lightly whisk the egg and set it aside. Brush the pumpkin balls with the egg wash and bake for 20 minutes, or until golden brown and fully cooked. Remove from the oven and immediately brush them with melted butter.

9. Let the buns cool for 30 minutes, then carefully cut the kitchen strings at the top and bottom of the pumpkin rolls. Gently remove and discard the strings. Place a pumpkin seed on each pumpkin roll.

10. Serve while warm and crispy on the outside!

TIP: *You may have to add less or more flour to your dough, depending on the flour quality.*

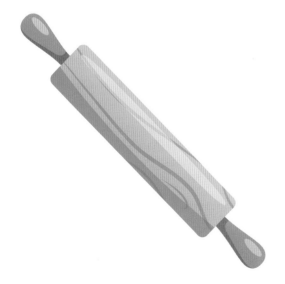

BLACK CAT ICEBOX SHORTBREAD COOKIES

FOR THE COOKIE DOUGH:

1¼ sticks butter, softened

1 cup powdered sugar

½ teaspoon salt

1 large egg

1 teaspoon vanilla extract

3 cups cake flour

4 tablespoons almond flour

black, pink, and purple food coloring

3 tablespoons dark cocoa powder

3 tablespoon milk, for assembling

FOR THE ROYAL ICING:

¼ cup powdered sugar

egg white from 1 egg

2 teaspoons lemon juice

STEP 8

STEP 10

These super-cute shortbread cookies undoubtedly resemble a certain black cat that once traveled to a seaside town with a young witch.

Yield: 30 cookies | Prep time: 1 hour | Cook time: 15 minutes

1. In a large mixing bowl of a stand mixer fitted with a paddle attachment, cream the butter and sugar on medium-high speed until the mixture becomes pale and creamy.

2. Add the salt, egg, and vanilla extract. Mix until combined.

3. Sift the cake flour and almond flour into the mixture. Mix on medium-low speed until well combined.

4. Reserve ⅓ of the dough in a small mixing bowl and add 1 to 2 drops of purple food coloring. Set aside.

5. For the remainder of the dough, add cocoa powder and 1 to 2 drops of the black food coloring. Mix using a spatula until well combined.

6. To shape the black cat, reserve ¼ of the black dough in a small bowl and set aside. For the remaining black dough, encase it in parchment paper and shape it into a cylinder. This will be the face. Make 2 small indents at the top where the cat's ears will go.

7. For the ears, divide the purple dough in half and shape 2 long pyramids using your hands.

8. Using the reserved black cookie dough, divide it in half and roll out as thin as possible. Encase the 2 purple pyramids in the black cookie dough and wrap them in parchment paper so they do not crack.

9. Place all the cookie dough in the refrigerator to chill for 15 to 30 minutes.

10. Take the cookie dough out of the refrigerator. To assemble the black cat cookies, attach the 2 pyramid shapes to the larger black cylinder (where the indents are) to make the ears. Use a bit of milk so they can be easily attached.

11. Preheat the oven to 350°F. Line 2 baking sheets with parchment paper or silicone mats.

STEP 12

STEP 13

12. Cut the cookies horizontally so they are ½-inch thick. This should yield 25 to 30 cookies.

13. Bake for 15 minutes or until they have firmed up, then let them cool for 5 minutes on the baking tray before transferring them to a wire rack to cool completely.

14. To make the royal icing, combine all the ingredients in a medium mixing bowl. Mix until well combined. In each of 2 separate bowls, reserve 2 tablespoons of the royal icing. Set aside the larger quantity of royal icing, as this will remain white. Add ½ drop of red food coloring to one bowl and 1 drop of black food coloring to the other bowl.

15. Pipe white eyes for the black cat using the white royal icing. Pipe black icing for the cat's pupils and pink icing for the nose.

RED BOW ICEBOX SHORTBREAD COOKIES

FOR THE COOKIE DOUGH:

1¼ sticks butter, softened

1 cup powdered sugar

½ teaspoon salt

1 large egg

1 teaspoon vanilla extract

3 cups cake flour

4 tablespoons almond flour

red food coloring

2 tablespoon milk, for assembling

¾ cup white royal icing

STEP 5

STEP 7

STEP 9

The only thing cuter than a black cat is a black cat with a red bow!

Yield: 40 bow cookies | Prep time: 1 hour | Cook time: 15 minutes

1. In a large mixing bowl using a stand mixer fitted with a paddle attachment, cream the butter and sugar on medium-high speed until the mixture becomes pale and creamy.

2. Add the salt, egg, and vanilla extract. Mix until combined.

3. Sift the cake flour and almond flour into the mixture. Mix on medium-low speed until well combined.

4. Add 1 to 3 drops of red food coloring to the cookie dough and mix with a silicone spatula until well combined.

5. To make the red bows, divide the red dough into thirds. Roll out the dough into 3 long cylinders. For 2 cylinders, pinch 1 end to a point, forming a teardrop shape. Encase the cookie dough in parchment paper.

6. Place all the cookie dough in the refrigerator to chill for 15 to 30 minutes.

7. To assemble the red bows, attach the 2 teardrop shapes to the cylinder. Return both cookies to the refrigerator and chill for an additional 30 minutes.

8. Preheat the oven to 350°F. Line 2 baking sheets with parchment paper or silicone mats.

9. Cut the cookies horizontally so they are ½-inch thick. This should yield 25 to 30 cookies.

10. Bake for 15 minutes or until they have firmed up, then let cool for 5 minutes on the baking tray before transferring them to a wire rack to cool completely.

11. To make the royal icing, you can follow the instructions on page 101. Pipe the royal icing along the borders of the red bow cookies. Enjoy them warm or at room temperature.

CURRY BREAD (KARE PAN)

1½ tablespoons superfine sugar

½ cup warm milk

1 teaspoon instant dry yeast

1¾ cups all-purpose flour

1 large egg

2 teaspoons neutral-flavored oil

½ teaspoon salt

FOR THE CURRY FILLING:
½ yellow onion, diced

2 tablespoons neutral-flavored oil

1 clove garlic, minced

1 teaspoon grated fresh ginger

¼ cup cubed carrots

½ pound ground beef

1½ cups water

¼ cup cubed potatoes

1 curry roux block

¼ cup peas

¼ cup chopped fresh cilantro leaves

1 teaspoon cayenne pepper

½ teaspoon salt

pepper, to taste

FOR BREADING AND FRYING:
1 egg

1 cup panko breadcrumbs

2 to 3 cups vegetable oil

Popular in Japanese bakeries, this curry bread will certainly be a family favorite with its savory filling, chewy texture, and light coating of crispy panko. To make the curry filling, I personally use the S&B Golden Curry roux block. However, use any curry roux block you have available

Yield: 8 servings | Prep time: 2 hours, 45 minutes | Cook time: 50 minutes

1. In a medium bowl, mix together the sugar and warm milk until the sugar has dissolved. Mix the yeast into the milk mixture and let sit for 5 to 10 minutes as the yeast activates and the mixture becomes frothy.

2. Using the dough hook attachment in a stand mixer set to low speed, combine the yeast mixture, flour, egg, oil, and salt until the mixture is well combined and a rough dough ball forms. Increase the speed to medium and knead for 5 to 7 minutes, until the dough is smooth and pliable. The dough will be slightly sticky but should be springy when you lightly press it with your thumb.

3. Place the dough in a greased bowl. Cover the bowl tightly with plastic wrap or a reusable silicone cover and let the dough rise in a warm place for 45 minutes to 1 hour, until it has doubled in size. The time may vary, depending on your weather conditions.

4. To make your curry filling, in a large pot or nonstick frying pan over medium heat, fry your onion in the oil until it has softened. This should take 5 minutes.

5. Add the garlic, ginger, and carrots, and sauté until the carrots have softened slightly, about 3 minutes.

6. Add the ground beef and fry until it has browned on all sides, approximately 7 minutes.

7. Add the water, potatoes, and curry roux block to the pot. Let it gently simmer for 15 minutes, until the curry starts to thicken and the potatoes are fully cooked.

8. Add the peas and let simmer for an additional 5 minutes.

9. Add the chopped cilantro leaves and the cayenne pepper for some heat. Season with salt and pepper, to taste. Set aside to cool. The curry should be thick enough to fill your buns without being runny. If needed, you can cook the curry down for an additional 5 to 10 minutes, until the water has evaporated.

STEP 10

STEP 11A

STEP 11B

STEP 13

STEP 14

10. Once the dough has risen, place it onto a floured working surface and gently punch/press it down. Divide the dough into 8 equal portions and lightly knead each portion for 1 minute. Form each piece into a ball and let them rest on a baking sheet for 30 minutes in a warm place.

11. Using a rolling pin, roll out the first ball into a flat disk around ¼-inch thick, (it should not be too thin). Thin out the edges with your fingers. Place 1 tablespoon of the curry mixture in the thicker center of the circle and fold the dough in half while encasing the curry mixture. Seal the edges by tightly pinching them. Finally, fold the edges over to ensure the filling will not burst out during the proofing and frying process. Repeat with the remainder of the dough balls.

12. Prepare your breading station by whisking an egg in a bowl and pouring the panko breadcrumbs onto a plate.

13. Place a curry bun in the whisked eggs and coat it well. Place it in the panko breadcrumbs and coat it all over, then transfer it to a baking tray. Continue with the rest of the buns, then let them rest for an additional 30 minutes, until they almost double in size. If you place a finger in the dough, the indentation should remain.

14. To deep fry the bread, heat the oil in a frying pot to 395°F. Sprinkle a bit of the panko breadcrumbs into the oil. If it sizzles, the oil is ready. Place 2 to 3 curry buns in the oil, seam side down. After a few seconds, flip the buns over so their seam side is up. Constantly turn the buns until they are fully cooked and have turned golden brown. You can make a small incision with a knife or use a toothpick to ensure that the dough is fully cooked (that is, the dough is not runny). Transfer the buns to a wire rack to drain while cooling. It should take 5 to 8 minutes to cook the buns.

Enjoy hot or at room temperature.

TIP: *Try not to overfill your buns with the curry mixture while folding, as this will become a problem when you are frying later.*

TIP: *These fry relatively quickly, so be sure they do not burn. For a healthier alternative, you can place the curry buns in the oven for 10 to 15 minutes at 375°F and bake until golden brown.*

TIP: *Keep the leftovers in an airtight container and store in the refrigerator for 3 days or in the freezer for 3 to 4 weeks. To reheat, bake at 350°F until warm inside.*

RED BEAN CROISSANT

FOR THE YEAST MIXTURE:
½ cup plus 2 tablespoons warm milk

1 teaspoon superfine sugar

2 teaspoons instant dry yeast

FOR THE DOUGH:
2½ cups bread flour

¼ teaspoon salt

1 egg yolk

⅓ cup superfine sugar

2 tablespoons melted butter

FOR THE BEURRAGE, OR BUTTER BLOCK:
5 ounces softened butter

FOR THE FILLING:
⅓ cup red bean paste (see the Red Bean Bao recipe on page 95 if you want to make this from scratch)

1 egg, whisked

STEP 5

STEP 7

Inspired by the baked snacks distributed by a famous broomstick delivery service, these super-flaky, buttery croissants are to die for, with an Asian twist of sweet red bean filling oozing out of the center.

Yield: 6 croissants | Prep time: 2 days | Cook time: 20 minutes

1. Add the warm milk and sugar to a small bowl and mix until well combined. Add the yeast to the water-sugar mixture and stir. Leave the bowl in a warm, draft-free location until the mixture becomes frothy (similar to the froth in a cappuccino). This should take between 2 to 10 minutes in warm weather; however, this depends on the weather conditions. Please see the tip box for more advice.

2. To make the dough, sift the flour and salt into a large mixing bowl. Mix until combined. Make a well in the center and add the activated yeast, egg yolk, sugar, and melted butter. Stir with a wooden spoon until it forms a rough dough. Using the palm of your hands, knead the dough until it fully comes together.

3. To strengthen the gluten in the dough, pick up the dough, throw it against the table, and fold it over itself. Repeat until the surface of the dough becomes smooth, about 1 minute.

4. Shape the dough into a ball and place it in a medium bowl. Cover with plastic wrap or a reusable silicone cover and let it rest in the refrigerator for 10 minutes.

5. Pull the edge of the chilled dough and gently stretch, then fold it over itself. Gently pat it down with the palm of your hand. Repeat the process for the entire perimeter of the dough until all sides have been stretched. Flip the dough, ensuring the seam side is facing down, and refrigerate for another 10 minutes. Be careful not to tear the dough during the stretching process.

6. After 10 minutes, repeat step 5. Place the dough back in the bowl and let it rest in the refrigerator for 30 minutes.

7. On a 12 x 16-inch sheet of parchment paper, using a pencil, lightly draw a 7 x 7-inch square in the center of the sheet. Place the chilled dough in the center of the drawn square and fold the sides of the parchment paper over it, encasing the dough.

STEP 8

STEP 12

STEP 14

STEP 16A

STEP 16B

8. Flip the parcel over (edges side down) and gently roll the edges of the dough, molding it to the shape of the parchment paper. Make sure the dough is evenly rolled out.

9. Place the parcel in the refrigerator and let it chill overnight or for at least 12 hours.

10. For the *beurrage*, or butter block, on a 12 x 13-inch sheet of parchment paper, draw a 4 x 4-inch square on the sheet, using a pencil. Place the block of butter in the center and fold the edges of the parchment paper to encase the butter. Flip the parcel over (edges side down) and gently roll the butter so it spreads to the edges of the square parcel. Place it in the refrigerator and chill for 15 to 25 minutes.

11. Take the dough out of the parchment paper parcel. Lightly dust a work surface with flour and place the chilled dough in the center. Using a rolling pin, roll out the dough, elongating the corners and roughly forming a 6 x 6-inch square.

12. Place your butter block diagonally (looks like a diamond) in the center of your dough. Take each edge of the dough and stretch it over the butter, encasing it. Seal the butter in the dough by pinching the edges and flipping the dough, seam side down.

13. Lightly flour the rolling pin and press down on the dough multiple times along its the entire length. This helps encase the butter. With even pressure, roll the dough into a roughly 18-inch-long rectangle.

14. With the short edges of the rectangular dough facing toward you, grab the bottom of the dough and fold it over itself ¾ of the way up the rectangle. Take the top half and fold it the remaining ¼ of the way until both ends meet evenly. Lightly pat down so they stick. Fold the dough in half (the longer portion over the short portion), making an envelope shape. Finally, lightly tap down the dough so the layers are compressed and stuck together.

15. Wrap the dough in plastic wrap and let it rest in the fridge for 1 hour.

16. Roll the chilled dough with even pressure on a lightly floured surface in the same direction, shaping it into an 18 x 7-inch-long rectangle Fold it ⅓ of the way down, then fold the bottom part so that it overlaps evenly on the other side.

STEP 20

STEP 22A

STEP22B

STEP 22C

STEP 23

17. Wrap in plastic wrap and place in the fridge for 1 to 12 hours.

18. For the final roll, roll the dough into a wider and thicker 10 x 10-inch square.

19. Create marks with a knife at the bottom of the dough at 1½-inch intervals. Repeat for the top part of the dough.

20. To cut the croissant, make long triangular cuts, using the markings as a guide. This should yield 5 to 6 croissant triangles.

21. Preheat the oven to 400°F. Line 2 baking sheets with parchment paper or silicone mats.

22. Take a triangle of dough and gently elongate it to make it 1 inch longer. Place 1 to 2 teaspoons of red bean paste in the center of the triangular dough and roll the dough up very tightly, starting from the longer end up to the point of the triangle. Repeat this process with every croissant.

23. Place the croissants tail-side down on the lined baking sheet and brush the tops with egg wash. Cover with an inverted rimmed baking sheet and let rest at 78°F for 2 hours.

24. Once the croissants have roughly doubled in size, bake at 400°F for 6 minutes. Then, bake again at 330°F for 10 to 15 minutes, or until they're golden brown and puffy.

25. Serve warm or at room temperature, with some coffee.

TIP: *Please refer to my tip box in the Red Bean Bao recipe on page 97 if you are struggling to get your dough to rise.*

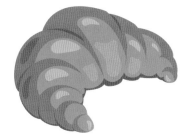

MINI SWEDISH PRINCESS CAKE

FOR THE SPONGE CAKE:
1¼ cups cake flour

½ cup almond flour

1 teaspoon baking powder

¼ teaspoon salt

4 large eggs

¾ cup superfine sugar

½ cup butter, melted

FOR THE PASTRY CREAM:
½ cup sugar

½ cup flour

¼ cup corn flour/cornstarch

1 teaspoon salt

3 large egg yolks

2 cups whole milk

½ cup cold butter, cubed

2 teaspoons vanilla extract

FOR THE WHIPPED CREAM:
2½ teaspoons unflavored gelatin powder

2 tablespoons warm water

2 cups whipping cream

¼ cup powdered sugar

1 teaspoon vanilla extract

FOR THE RASPBERRY JAM:
1 cup raspberries

¾ cup superfine sugar

FOR THE DECORATION:
9 ounces white fondant

red and mint-green food coloring

powdered sugar, for dusting

Hailing from a famous seaside bakery with a Swedish influence, this Mini-Swedish Princess Cake is a beautifully decorated cake with layers of vanilla sponge, raspberry jam, whipped cream, and vanilla custard.

Yield: 6 sponge cakes | Prep time: 1 hour, 30 minutes, plus 4 hours to overnight to chill | Cook time: 25 minutes

FOR THE SPONGE CAKE
1. Preheat the oven to 350°F.

2. Combine the flour, almond flour, baking powder, and salt in a medium bowl and set aside.

3. Using a stand mixer, beat the eggs and sugar on high speed until the mixture is pale and thickened. Gently fold the dry ingredients into your egg mixture. Add the melted butter and stir until well combined.

4. Pour the batter in a greased 9 x 13-inch baking pan and bake for 10 to 15 minutes, until golden brown and springy. Let the cake completely cool on a wire rack.

5. Using a 3-inch cake ring or a round cookie cutter, cut out 12 circles. Set aside.

FOR THE PASTRY CREAM
1. Combine the sugar, flour, corn flour or cornstarch, salt, egg yolks, and milk in a medium pot. Transfer the pot to a stove over medium heat and whisk the mixture constantly.

2. Add the butter in 3 batches and continue to stir until it has melted. Add the vanilla extract and whisk for 5 to 7 minutes, until the mixture starts to thicken and coats the back of a spoon.

3. Remove pot from heat and let the mixture cool. Once it has cooled slightly, press a sheet of plastic wrap over the surface of the pastry cream and place it in the refrigerator to chill for an 1 hour.

FOR THE WHIPPED CREAM

1. Combine the gelatin powder and water in a small bowl. Mix until the powder has dissolved completely.

2. Place the whipping cream in the bowl of a stand mixer with a whip attachment. Beat at medium speed until soft peaks form.

3. Gradually add the gelatin mixture and powdered sugar to the whipped cream while the mixer is running.

4. Add the vanilla extract, increase the mixer speed to high, and beat until stiff peaks form. Set aside.

FOR THE RASPBERRY JAM

1. Mash the raspberries using a potato masher. Combine the raspberries with the sugar in a small saucepan over medium-high heat. Bring to a boil and stir continuously, until the berries have broken down and the mixture has thickened. This takes about 5 to 7 minutes.

2. Place the raspberry jam through a fine-mesh sieve into a medium bowl. Let it cool to room temperature and set aside.

TO ASSEMBLE THE CAKE

1. Place 1 round cake layer on a plate or cake board. Use a spoon to spread 1 tablespoon of the raspberry jam and 1 tablespoon of the pastry cream onto the cake layer. Top with a second cake piece.

2. Add 3 to 4 tablespoons of whipped cream on top of the cake layer and smooth into a dome shape using a large spatula. Repeat for the other mini princess cakes. Refrigerate the mini princess cakes for at least 3 hours or overnight to firm up the pastry cream.

3. While the cakes chill, dust a work surface for the fondant. Knead the fondant with your hands until it softens slightly and is easier to roll out.

4. Reserve ¼ of the fondant and add 1 to 2 drops of red food coloring to the reserved fondant. Knead until the fondant has turned a light pink and set aside. Lightly add powdered sugar as needed to prevent sticking.

5. Add 3 to 4 drops of the mint-green food coloring to the remainder of the white fondant and knead until the color is evenly distributed.

6. Roll the mint-green fondant into a large circle, adding powdered sugar underneath to prevent it from sticking. Gently place the rolled-out fondant over the top of a chilled cake. Use the palm of your hands to form it to the shape the cake. Trim the excess fondant from the bottom of the cake using a pizza cutter or pastry wheel. Gently tuck the bottom edges of the fondant under the cake. Repeat for the remainder of the princess cakes.

7. To make the fondant rose, shape a thumbnail-size teardrop shape. Dust your work surface with powdered sugar, roll out the remaining pink fondant as thin as possible, and cut out 5 smaller oval shapes using a cookie cutter or a sharp knife. These will form your rose petals.

8. Using a ball tool or a rolling pin, thin out the edges of the fondant petals, keeping the bottoms thick. This creates a slight ruffle.

9. To get the flower petals to stick to the teardrop-shaped fondant, slightly wet the petal with water using your hands. Wrap the petal around the cone with the pointy end facing upward. Wrap the other petals in the same manner, slightly overlapping the other petals. Gently pinch the edges and bend the layers outward as you add more petals. Set aside and allow for the rose to dry. Repeat this for the 5 other roses.

10. Attach the rose to the top center of the cake using pastry cream or a dot of honey. Dust the top of the cake with powdered sugar using a small sieve before serving.

TIP: *Try to buy good-quality fondant as it will have a lower tendency to crack and crumble when covering the mini Swedish princess cakes.*

TIP: *To keep the fondant rose petals from drying out, cover them with plastic wrap or a bowl turned upside down.*

MINI SWEDISH ALMOND COFFEE CAKE

FOR THE SPONGE CAKE:

4 egg whites

¼ cup plus 2 tablespoons superfine sugar

2 tablespoons lemon juice

1 teaspoon instant coffee

pinch of salt

1 cup plus 2 tablespoons ground almonds

FOR THE BUTTERCREAM:

4 egg yolks

½ cup heavy cream

¼ cup plus 2 tablespoons sugar

1 teaspoon vanilla extract

½ cup plus 1 tablespoon unsalted butter, softened

sliced almonds, for decorating

Sandwiched between rich buttercream and covered in toasted sliced almonds, this beautiful Swedish cake is very light and gluten-free, with a subtle hint of coffee. Best enjoyed after a long day at work, even if you don't work part-time at a seaside bakery.

Yield: 1 to 2 servings | Prep time: 1 hour, 30 minutes, plus 1 hour to chill | Cook time: 45 minutes

1. Preheat the oven to 350°F.

2. In a medium bowl using a stand mixer with a whisk attachment, beat the egg whites, sugar, lemon juice, coffee, and salt until stiff peaks form. Gently fold the ground almonds into the meringue. Place the batter in 2 (6-inch) baking pans and bake for 20 to 25 minutes, or until a toothpick inserted in the center of the cake comes out clean.

3. To make the buttercream, whisk the egg yolks in a bowl and set aside.

4. In a medium pot, bring the cream and sugar to a simmer, about 5 minutes. Remove from the heat, and set aside.

5. Pour the hot cream mixture to the egg yolks in a thin stream while whisking constantly. Try not to scramble the eggs.

6. Transfer the egg mixture back to the pot and simmer for 5 to 10 minutes, until it coats the back of the spoon. Make sure to constantly whisk the mixture.

7. Remove the pot from the heat and stir in the vanilla extract. Transfer the mixture to a medium bowl, cover, and chill in the refrigerator for 1 hour.

8. In a large bowl using a stand mixer with a whisk attachment, beat the softened butter until smooth. Gradually add the chilled egg mixture on medium speed (about 2 to 3 tablespoon at a time) and whisk until combined. Set aside.

9. In a small pan, toast the sliced almonds until golden brown, about 3 minutes. Set aside to cool at room temperature.

10. To frost the cakes, layer ½ inch of the buttercream on top of the first cake. Add the other cake layer on top and spread enough buttercream to cover the entire cake. Gently place the toasted sliced almonds over the entire cake. Let it chill in the fridge for at least 1 hour before serving.

11. Serve chilled or at room temperature.

SWEDISH CARDAMOM BUNS

FOR THE BREAD DOUGH:

½ cup warm whole milk

3 tablespoons sugar

1 teaspoon instant dry yeast

3 cups bread flour

½ teaspoon salt

⅓ cup salted butter, softened and cubed

2 tablespoons water

FOR THE CARDAMOM FILLING:

½ cup brown sugar

⅓ cup butter, softened

2 teaspoons ground cardamom

FOR THE DECORATION:

1 large egg

3 tablespoons sugar pearls

1 tablespoon honey

1 tablespoon water

5 tablespoons pistachio nuts, shelled and roughly chopped

These fluffy buns are a unique fusion between a cinnamon roll and pull-apart bread. Very light, delicate, and packed with aromatic cardamom, the buns pair well with coffee or even some Hot Honeyed Milk (page 79).

Yield: 6 buns | Prep time: 45 minutes plus 2 hours, 15 minutes to rest | Cook time: 20 to 25 minutes

1. Combine the warm milk and sugar in a small bowl and whisk until the sugar has dissolved. Add the yeast to the milk-sugar mixture and stir. Leave the bowl in a warm, draft-free location until the mixture becomes frothy (similar to the froth in a cappuccino). This should take between 2 to 10 minutes, depending on the weather conditions.

2. Place the flour and salt in a large mixing bowl. Using a stand mixer with a dough hook attachment, mix until well combined. Add the yeast mixture to the flour and mix to form a soft dough. Tip onto a work surface and knead for 10 minutes, or run the freestanding mixer for 10 minutes, until the dough is smooth and stretchy.

3. Add the cubed butter to the dough mixture and knead for another 2 minutes. Place the dough back in the medium bowl, cover with plastic wrap, and let the dough rise in a warm environment for 1 hour and 45 minutes, or until it has doubled in size.

4. In a separate bowl, combine the sugar, butter, and ground cardamom. Set aside.

5. Knock the air out of the chilled dough, then roll it to a roughly 14 x 18-inch rectangle, with the longer edge facing you. Spread the cardamom butter over the entire surface, including the edges.

6. Fold the top ⅓ down to the middle and the bottom ⅓ up and over the 2 layers, like an envelope, so you have 3 layers of dough.

7. Cut the dough into 12 equal strips, measuring about 1½ x 4 inches each. For each strip, make a slit down the middle but be careful not to cut the entire strip completely at the edges (that is, the 2 edges should still be intact).

8. Twist each strip away from the center 2 or 3 times, then tie the dough in a knot and tuck the ends underneath the bun.

9. Line 2 baking trays with a silicone mat. Place the cardamom buns on the tray, covered with plastic wrap or an inverted baking tray, and leave in a warm place for 30 minutes to an hour or until they double in size.

10. Preheat the oven to 350°F.

11. Whisk the egg in a small bowl to make an egg wash. Brush the buns with the wash and sprinkle the sugar pearls on top. Bake the buns for 20 to 25 minutes, until golden brown. Turn the tray during the 15-minute mark for even browning.

12. In a small bowl, dissolve the honey in water. Once the buns are baked, transfer to a wire rack to cool. Brush the honey water over the buns and sprinkle some chopped pistachio nuts on top.

HAM AND CHEESE BREADSTICKS

FOR THE BREAD DOUGH:
¾ cup warm whole milk

2 tablespoons sugar

1½ teaspoons instant dry yeast

2½ cups bread flour

1 teaspoon salt

3 tablespoons butter, cubed

1 large egg

FOR THE FILLING:
3 tablespoons butter, softened

5 tablespoons fresh chopped parsley

6 slices ham, cut into thin ½-inch strips

1 cup shredded Gouda cheese

The ideal snack for when you're late to Aviation Club!

Yield: 12 breadsticks | Prep time: 1 hour, 30 minutes | Cook time: 25 to 30 minutes

1. Combine the warm milk and sugar in a small bowl and whisk until the sugar has dissolved. Add the yeast to the milk-sugar mixture and stir. Leave the bowl in a warm, draft-free location until the mixture becomes frothy (similar to the froth in a cappuccino). This should take between 2 to 10 minutes, depending on the weather conditions.

2. Place the flour and salt in a large mixing bowl. Using a stand mixer with a dough hook attachment, mix until well combined.

3. Add the yeast mixture, butter, and egg to the flour and mix to form a soft dough. Tip the dough onto a work surface and knead for 10 minutes, or run the freestanding mixer for 10 minutes, until the dough is smooth and stretchy. Place the dough back in the medium bowl, cover with plastic wrap, and let it rise in a warm environment for 1 hour, or until it has doubled in size.

4. To make the filling, in a small bowl, combine the butter and parsley and mix until the parsley is evenly distributed.

5. Preheat the oven to 350°F.

6. Tip the dough onto a floured work surface and with a rolling pin, roll it out into a roughly 11 x 15-inch rectangle.

7. Using a pizza cutter or a knife, slice the dough into 12 even strips. Place a slice of ham, shredded cheese, and the parsley butter onto the strips. Hold the end of each strip and twist in opposite directions to form twists. Place it on a lined baking sheet. Repeat for the remaining breadsticks.

8. Bake for 25 to 30 minutes, until the dough is golden brown.

9. Let them rest on the baking sheet for 5 minutes and transfer to a wire rack to cool down completely.

GREEN TEA MELON PAN STUFFED WITH BLUEBERRY COMPOTE

FOR THE BREAD DOUGH:

½ cup plus 3 tablespoons warm whole milk

2 tablespoons superfine sugar

1 teaspoon instant dry yeast

2 cups plus 3 tablespoons bread flour

1 teaspoon salt

1 large egg

3½ tablespoons butter, cubed

½ teaspoon good-quality matcha powder

FOR THE COOKIE DOUGH:

⅓ cup butter, softened

⅓ cup plus 2 tablespoons sugar

1 large egg

1 teaspoon vanilla extract

1½ cups plus 1 tablespoon flour

1 teaspoon matcha

1 teaspoon baking powder

2 tablespoons whole milk

5 tablespoons granulated brown sugar, for sprinkling

FOR THE BLUEBERRY FILLING:

2 cups frozen blueberries

3 tablespoons water

¼ granulated brown sugar

2 teaspoons lemon juice

1 teaspoon lemon zest

A twist on a classic Japanese sweet bread that visually resembles its namesake, this pastry is a thin layer of crisp biscuit/cookie crust packed with a zesty blueberry compote. Crunchy on the outside, soft and fluffy on the inside.

Yield: 10 servings, 1 bun per serving | Prep time: 2 hours, 45 minutes | Cook time: 30 minutes

1. Combine the warm milk and sugar in a small bowl and whisk until the sugar has dissolved. Add the yeast to the milk-sugar mixture and stir. Leave the bowl in a warm, draft-free location until the mixture becomes frothy (similar to the froth in a cappuccino). This should take between 2 to 10 minutes, depending on the weather conditions.

2. Place the flour and salt in a large mixing bowl. Using a stand mixer with a dough hook attachment, mix until well combined. Add the yeast mixture, and egg to the flour and mix to form a soft dough. Knead the dough hook for an additional 10 minutes on medium speed. While the dough is being kneaded, add in the cubed butter and matcha until the butter is combined and a smooth and silky dough forms.

3. Place the dough in a greased bowl, cover, and let rest for 1 hour, or until the dough has doubled in size.

4. While the dough is rising, make the cookie dough by creaming the butter and sugar in a bowl using the stand mixer on medium speed. This should take 5 minutes, or until the butter mixture is pale and creamy.

5. Add the egg and vanilla and mix until well combined. Slowly add the flour, matcha, and baking powder and whisk until well incorporated. Divide the cookie dough into 10 small balls and roll them out into 0.2-inch-thick disks. Set them aside in the fridge.

6. For the blueberry compote, combine the blueberries, water, sugar, lemon juice, and lemon zest in a medium pot. Cook over medium heat for 10 to 15 minutes, or until the compote becomes thick and sticky. Transfer it to a medium bowl and let it cool to room temperature.

7. Once the bread dough has doubled in size, divide it into 10 equal balls and knead on a lightly floured surface until smooth. Flatten each ball using a rolling pin, keeping the sides of the dough thinner than the center.

8. Place 1 tablespoon of the blueberry compote in the center of each circle of bread dough. Fold the edges of the bread dough over to enclose the blueberry filling and pinch to seal.

9. Take out the chilled cookie dough disks and place 1 on top of the bread dough while gently compressing the doughs together with your hands.

10. Make crosshatch/diagonal score marks on the cookie dough and sprinkle it with granulated brown sugar. Repeat for the remaining buns.

11. Place the buns on a lined baking tray and cover with an inverted baking tray or plastic wrap. Let them rest in a warm place for 40 minutes, or until they double in size.

12. Preheat the oven to 350°F.

13. Once the buns have doubled in size, place them in the oven and bake for 15 minutes.

14. Serve warm or at room temperature.

JAPANESE SOUFFLÉ CHEESECAKE

⅓ cup cream cheese, room temperature

2 tablespoons butter

¼ cup whole milk

3 large eggs, whites and yolks separated

5 tablespoons cake flour

2½ teaspoons cornstarch

1 teaspoon lemon zest

1 teaspoon vanilla extract

1 teaspoon lemon juice

¼ cup superfine sugar

powdered sugar, strawberries, and blueberries, for decorating

This fluffy and moist soufflé cheesecake is very popular in Japan, with its delicate and creamy texture that melts in your mouth. Try not to eat half of this cake in one sitting!

Yield: 6 to 8 servings, 1 slice per serving | Prep time: 45 minutes | Cook time: 50 minutes to 1 hour, plus 2 hours to chill

1. Preheat the oven to 325°F. Line a 9-inch cake pan with parchment paper along the bottom and sides. Cover the outside of the pan with a large piece of aluminum foil.

2. In a medium bowl, combine the cream cheese, butter, and milk. Place the bowl over a pot of simmering water (known as a *bain-marie*) ensuring that the bottom of the bowl does not touch the water. Make sure that your bowl is larger than the pot and the edges of the pot will hold the bowl in place. Heat the mixture to 140°F, or until it's melted and smooth.

3. Take the mixture off the heat and add the egg yolks. Whisk until combined.

4. Add the sifted cake flour, cornstarch, lemon zest, and vanilla extract, and stir. Set aside.

5. In a separate medium bowl, add lemon juice to the egg whites. Using an electric beater, whisk the egg whites to soft peaks while adding the sugar in 3 intervals. Beat until stiff peaks form.

6. Using a silicone spatula, fold the egg white mixture into the flour mixture until well incorporated. Do not overmix.

7. Pour the batter into a pan and place it in a deep tray. Using a toothpick, make a zigzag motion in the batter to remove any air bubbles. Pour hot water into the tray, about 1-inch deep.

8. Place the cake pan into the preheated oven and bake for 10 minutes. Then, lower the temperature to 300°F and bake for an additional 40 to 50 minutes. The cheesecake is ready when a toothpick inserted into the center comes out clean.

9. Remove and place the cake pan onto a cooling rack. Let it sit to cool and then chill the cake in the fridge for over 2 hours. Gently remove the soufflé cheesecake from the pan and remove the parchment paper. Place the cheesecake onto a cutting board and decorate with powdered sugar, strawberries, and blueberries. Serve chilled.

TIP: *I try to use both parchment paper and cooking spray to ensure that the cheesecake does not stick to the pan. Alternatively, you can grease the pan with additional butter.*

TIP: *Use a dampened knife to make clean cuts to the cheesecake.*

CONVERSIONS

Volume

U.S.	U.S. Equivalent	Metric
1 tablespoon (3 teaspoons)	½ fluid ounce	15 milliliters
¼ cup	2 fluid ounces	60 milliliters
⅓ cup	3 fluid ounces	90 milliliters
½ cup	4 fluid ounces	120 milliliters
⅔ cup	5 fluid ounces	150 milliliters
¾ cup	6 fluid ounces	180 milliliters
1 cup	8 fluid ounces	240 milliliters
2 cups	16 fluid ounces	480 milliliters

Weight

U.S.	Metric
½ ounce	15 grams
1 ounce	30 grams
2 ounces	60 grams
¼ pound	115 grams
⅓ pound	150 grams
½ pound	225 grams
¾ pound	350 grams
1 pound	450 grams

Temperature

Fahrenheit (°F)	Celsius (°C)	Fahrenheit (°F)	Celsius (°C)
70°F	20°C	220°F	105°C
100°F	40°C	240°F	115°C
120°F	50°C	260°F	125°C
130°F	55°C	280°F	140°C
140°F	60°C	300°F	150°C
150°F	65°C	325°F	165°C
160°F	70°C	350°F	175°C
170°F	75°C	375°F	190°C
180°F	80°C	400°F	200°C
190°F	90°C	425°F	220°C
200°F	95°C	450°F	230°C

RECIPE INDEX

A

Almond coffee cakes, 114–115

B

Ba Wan (Crystal Skin Taiwanese
    Dumpling), 49–50
Bacon and eggs, 11
Bakery Treats, 78–123
Beef stew, 45
Bento boxes, 22–23, 24–25
Black Cat Icebox Shortbread Cookies, 100–101
Breadsticks, 119
Breakfast over Yokohama Port, 16
Breakfast recipes, 9–18

C

Cantonese egg cake, 87
Cardamom buns, 116–118
Cheese and Onion Fish Crackers, 88
Cheese and onion sandwich, 26
Chicken Congee "Okayu," 42
Chicken Karaage, 71
Chocolate cake, 81–83
Chorizo Spaghetti Bolognese, 40–41
Classic Tempura Selection, 52–53
Congee, 42
Crispy Pork Gyoza, 68–69
Crystal Skin Taiwanese Dumpling
    (Ba Wan), 49–50
Curry Bread (Kare Pan), 103–105

D

Date Night Pan-Seared Salmon in
    Beurre Blanc Sauce, 38–39
Decadent Hot Mocha, 18

Desserts, 78–123
Dinner recipes, 32–50
Duo Thumbprint Cookies, 91–92

E

Egg on toast, 12

G

Grandma's Herring and Pumpkin Pot Pie, 33, 35
Green Tea Melon Pan Stuffed with
    Blueberry Compote, 120–121
Gyoza, 68–69

H

Haaaaaaaam Ramen, 21
Ham and Cheese Breadsticks, 119
Ham sandwich, 20
Hearty Beef Stew to Feed a Crowd, 45
Hot Honeyed Milk, 79

I

Icebox shortbread cookies, 100–101, 102
Iconic School Lunch Bento, 22–23

J

Japanese Cream Stew, 46–47
Japanese Souffle Cheesecake, 122–123

K

Karaage, 71
Kare Pan (curry bread), 103, 105
Katsu, 59–60
Katsudon, 76

L

Lunch recipes, 19–31

M

Mackerel Braised in Miso, 31
Menchi Katsu, 59–60
Mini jelly, 86
Mini Swedish Almond Coffee Cake, 114–115
Mini Swedish Princess Cake, 111–113
Miso soup, 17
Mocha, 18
Morning Miso Soup, 17

O

Okayu, 42
Okonomiyaki, 72
On-the-Go Ham Sandwich, 20
Onigiri, 56, 58
Open-Faced Cheese and Onion Sandwich, 26

P

Pancakes, 15
Pot pie, 33–35
Princess cakes, 111–113
Pumpkin Bread, 98–99

R

Ramen, 21
Red Bean Bao, 95–97
Red Bean Croissant, 106–109
Red Bow Icebox Shortbread Cookies, 102
Rewarding and Decadent Chocolate Cake, 81–83

S

Sashimi platter, 28–29
"Save Our Building" School Bento, 24–25

Seaside Seafood Sashimi Platter, 28–29
Secret Message Fried Mackerel, 36
Shortbread cookies, 100–101, 102
Siberia Cake, 93–94
Skillet Bacon and Eggs, 11
Smoky and Sweet Yakitori, 61–62
Snack recipes, 51–77
Souffle cheesecake, 122–123
Spritz cookies, 85–86
Street food recipes, 51–77
Swedish almond coffee cake, 114–115
Swedish Cardamom Buns, 116–118
Swedish princess cake, 111–113

T

Takoyaki, 63–64
Tea Party Cantonese Egg Cake, 87
Tea Party Mini Gelatin, 86
Tea Party Spritz Cookies, 85–86
Tempura Rice Bowl (Ten-don), 55
Tempura, 52–53
Ten-don (Tempura Rice Bowl), 55
Thyme-Infused Egg on Toast, 12
Tonkatsu, 75
Trio of Onigiri, 56–58
Tuna Fish Crackers (for Your Feline Friends), 90

W

Witch-Delivered Bakery Treats, 98–123
A Witch's Secret to Magical Fluffy Pancakes, 15

Y

Yakisoba Pan, 65–67
Yakitori, 61–62

ACKNOWLEDGMENTS

Special thanks to Casie Vogel and the Ulysses Press team who have been guiding me through this cookbook journey and turning my dream into a reality. I would also like to express my gratitude to my mom, Edith Yun, who has been my moral support throughout this entire journey and has been helping me around the kitchen developing these recipes.

Finally, I would like to thank specifically Matthew Yun, Crystal Yun, Avon Singh, Sharon Obisi-Orlu, Nikita Haripersad, Claudeen Govender, and Yasser Mohammad. A further thank you to family, friends, work colleagues, and those who truly believed in my cooking. Finally, a special shout-out to those who were part of the taste-testing process; your constructive criticism has made these recipes even better!

ABOUT THE AUTHOR

Jessica Ann Yun is an epidemiologist by day and a part-time food blogger by night. Her food journey started in 2019, when she began showcasing her creative, innovative, and unique cooking style on her Instagram food blog. Gastronomy is one of her passions, and Jessica often finds cooking as a stress-reducing outlet when she needs a break from the public health realm. Her debut cookbook, *The Unofficial Studio Ghibli Cookbook*, transforms iconic food scenes from popular Japanese and Studio Ghibli films into reality. A Chinese South African who lives in Johannesburg, South Africa, Jessica creates new recipes and appreciates food that has no borders. You can follow more of her culinary journey on Instagram @jaysing.flavours.

photograph © Edith Yun